THE FIRST
12
MONTHS

THE FIRST 12 MONTHS

A COMPLETE START-UP GUIDE FOR ENTREPRENEURS

DAVID H BANGS

KOGAN
PAGE

First published in 1989 in the United States of America
by Upstart Publishing Company Inc, Portsmouth, New Hampshire 03801, USA.

This edition first published in Great Britain in 1991 by
Kogan Page Limited.

Kogan Page Limited
120 Pentonville Road
London N1 9JN

British Library Cataloguing in Publication Data
A CIP record for this book is available from the
British Library.

British Library.

ISBN 0-7494-0417-5
ISBN 0-7494-0262-8 Pbk

Typeset by DP Photosetting, Aylesbury, Bucks
Printed and bound in Great Britain by
Martins of Berwick, Berwick upon Tweed

◀ CONTENTS ▶

◀ INTRODUCTION ▶

To give you an idea of where you stand as a start-up entrepreneur, consider these figures:

- The latest figures published by the Registrar of Companies show that there are now some 1,112,000 limited companies in the United Kingdom. Independent research indicates that 70 per cent of these are family owned or family controlled.

- Customs and Excise statistics indicate that one and a half million businesses were registered for Value Added Tax in 1988, of which 64,000 were then new.

The survival rate is harder to quantify. The worst estimates indicate that around three out of five new businesses fail in the first five years. Some of these closures are more properly 'career changes' as no money is lost and the disappearance of the business (by closing the doors, merging, or changing to a different kind of business) is voluntary. Franchised businesses tend to do better, as they start off with the franchisor's expertise and back-up services in a tried and tested formula.

This book is directed to that larger segment of entrepreneurs – those of you who are planning to succeed in business. My credentials as author come from 20 years of small business experience and surviving most of the mistakes newcomers to small business ownership tend to make. In 1977, I started my own small business. It was a fairly typical start-up:

undercapitalised; uncertain about markets, products, and pricing; touch and go for the first few years.

Its survival is also typical. Most small businesses will succeed, provided their owners are determined, stubborn, and willing to take control of those variables that can be controlled. Changes in markets, competition, products, and customer perceptions are inevitable. Small businesses that can adapt to such changes because of their owners' foresight and careful planning will profit. Companies that become rigid won't make it.

A business owner who fails to plan, plans to fail. I believe this cliché and have noticed time and again that small business owners who take the time to think through their strategies, use information to balance their enthusiasm, and are smart enough to recognise their own limitations don't fail. A formal, written business plan is a great tool for controlling a business and maintaining focus – but I've also seen very successful businesses where the owner keeps the plan in his or her head. Because none of us is immortal, however, this risk is unnecessary. Entrepreneurs face plenty of risks as it is without adding to the list. A written business plan is helpful in so many ways that the time and effort to write and update it are trifling in comparison with the benefits it gives.

Since the process of starting a business is long and complex, be aware of the benefits of allowing yourself the full time (or longer) that this book suggests. Spending six months to a year before making one of the biggest investments you'll every make (both financial and personal) gives you time to modify your initial ideas, acquire the skills and information that will set your business apart from the ordinary, and ensure your success. Potentially disastrous management errors such as undercapitalisation, negative cash flow, poor recruitment, and choosing the wrong location can and should be avoided. For example, in a US Small Business Administration survey the most common answer to the question 'Why did you choose this location?' was 'Noticed vacancy'. Since location makes or breaks most retail and hospitality businesses, no wonder so many small business owners have a tough time.

Take your time. If you can, work for someone else for a while to learn the ins and outs of your kind of business. Take courses to improve your management skills. Keep a notebook with ideas about your products' benefits, the markets you plan to serve, the competition, and any other scrap of information that might give you a competitive advantage. Jot down ideas about how to serve your new boss (that is, your customers or clients) better than anyone else. What kind of prices will you charge? What level of after-sales service would make sense for your business?

Most important of all, make sure that meeting the demands of business ownership is consistent with your other goals in life. Small business can make you rich, but that may not be worth the dedication such a goal calls for. You have to balance your business and personal goals, or you won't attain either.

Good luck with your venture. I hope you'll find owning your business as exciting and rewarding as I have.

David H Bangs
Portsmouth, New Hampshire

◀ CHAPTER 1 ▶

THE BASICS OF BUSINESS OWNERSHIP

You can do it. You can be one of the thousands of people who will start a successful business during the next 12 months. This book will help you to set up and follow a process which will culminate in establishing the right business for you, based on your interests, goals and resources.

You can be one of the thousands of people who will start a successful business during the next 12 months.

It will take hard work; the most this process can do is to show you directions, pose questions and suggest ways to arrive at the answers. You have to provide the detailed answers, and in the process you will learn a lot about whether or not you should be in business for yourself.

Chapters 2 to 7 contain action plans to help you organise your time and use it effectively and purposefully. Some of the suggested actions can only be carried out by you; others should be carried out with the help of others; some can only be performed by experts, those professionals whom experienced business owners make sure of having in their teams. The suggested actions should be taken in sequence, but you may have special talents or experience which will help you to shorten the cycle by combining various steps. You may choose to ignore or minimise some of the actions. That's up to you, but you do so at your peril. For example, you may not feel you have the time or opportunity to work for someone else and gain experience in your proposed line of business. Ideally, you should work for such a business for a year or so in a management capacity, but you may have experience that is equivalent, or perhaps you can find courses or workshops to speed up your learning and experience.

Before starting the process, ask yourself some tough questions about your fitness to own and operate a business. Business ownership is an entrepreneur's dream, but it is not right for everyone. Qualities that can make the difference between success and failure include perseverance, stamina (emotional as well as physical) and the energy only the owner provides, courage to see you through difficult times, the ability to make decisions on incomplete knowledge, communication skills and willingness to take limited (not careless) risks. Not everyone has these qualities.

Successful business people seek out and follow the best advice they can.

You needn't be a genius to have a profitable start-up. You do need common sense, and should be willing to face and accept your own limitations. Successful business people seek out and follow the best advice they can. Refusal to do this is a good way to guarantee failure and is not evidence of strength of character. Outside advisers help you to make decisions based on facts, not wishful thinking, provide a reality check, and can give you insights that help your business to run better. This is particularly helpful in the pre-start-up phase, because you probably don't know what questions to ask. This book poses some questions, but each business and each location will present specific questions that no book, no matter how detailed, could anticipate.

The six myths of business ownership

Business ownership is surrounded by myths. Don't fall for the following, which are common and dangerous:

1. I can do it on a shoestring. Undercapitalisation (too little money invested in the business) is the biggest cause of small business failure and usually results in negative cash flow (more going out than coming in). While you may indeed be able to run a very tight ship, why take the risk when you can calculate the amount of capital investment needed to make your venture succeed? This cash reserve makes you sleep better, helps to avoid panicky decisions, and gives you the breathing room needed to run your business.

2. I can start living off the business immediately. Forget it. Most business owners find that it takes between six months and a year before their business can pay them a decent wage. Early expenses always outrun early revenues. For this reason alone, consider starting your business as a part-time or weekend venture if possible, or be prepared to live on savings (or other sources of income) until your business can afford to pay you. Home-based companies are a good way to start, as you can minimise your cash needs. This kind of economy is highly recommended, but of course doesn't fit all businesses.

3. I'll be my own boss.   Not likely! The business and its customers will be your boss and keep you occupied 60 or more hours a week. Your other bosses include employees, suppliers, bankers and investors.

4. I'll get rich overnight.   You won't. The get-rich-quick stories are either bogus (the many years of preparation are hidden) or so unusual that your chances of winning the pools are higher. Small businesses are a good way to build wealth, but it takes time. More than a third of businesses which grow significantly don't do so until they've been active for ten or more years.

Small businesses are a good way to build wealth; but it takes time.

5. I have nothing to lose. I'll incorporate and use other people's money.   Nonsense. The 'corporate shield' exists only in rare cases where the business is strongly capitalised and big enough to make creditors (suppliers, bankers, investors) rest easy. Start-ups seldom meet these criteria. The same applies to using OPM (Other People's Money), in spite of all the books and articles urging you to borrow your way to wealth. It isn't that easy to find OPM – and it seldom makes business sense to take on a debt if you can avoid it.

6. It takes money to make money.   This it a half-truth. Good business ideas attract money; bad ones don't, and shouldn't. There are businesses where the hurdle to entry is so high that substantial capital is needed. Printing, for example, or most manufacturing businesses call for so great an investment in machinery, plant and equipment that to all intents and purposes it does take money to make money. Many businesses don't have such high barriers to entry: service businesses, some retail businesses, some wholesale or distribution businesses fit this low capital criterion. If you lack capital, you should try to find such a business. People have made fortunes in all kinds of businesses.

How to reduce the risks of a start-up

The following are proven ways of lowering the inherent risks of starting a business, and are worth incorporating in your start-up plans:

- **Gain experience in management and in the type of business you plan to start.** Experience is not the only way to learn, but it is still the best teacher. Combine experience with course work, study and participation in trade associations, and you have an almost unbeatable start towards business success.

- **Plan ahead.** The action orientation many entrepreneurs pride themselves on has to be tempered with foresight and careful planning. A written business plan is inexpensive insurance. It will help you to focus on the important parts of your business, use your resources wisely and consistently, and save a lot of trouble.

- **Make sure you have your family's support.** Even though you're not devoting 168 hours a week to your business, your family will think you are. If your family understands and is willing to provide the emotional support you'll need during the start-up period, your chances improve dramatically. The impact of uncertain income, demands on your time and attention that will preoccupy you 24 hours a day for months at a stretch, and the sheer anxiety of being the responsible owner of a small business, put strains on the best relationships.

- **Be prepared to become tired and discouraged and still persevere.** It goes with the package. Stamina is important; so is persistence, because when things get tough (and they will) it's very easy to give up. Experts like to talk about the 'five-yard-line phenomenon', in which a business owner presses on and on against huge odds, gets discouraged and gives up or makes a stupid mistake when the goalpost is within reach. Starting a business from scratch is hard. You (and you alone) have to provide the impetus to get things going and keep them going. You don't have the built-in momentum of an existing business. The consistent injection of energy can become draining, but you have to keep it up.

- **Use facts to substantiate your insights and hunches before acting on them.** Decisions based on facts are far more likely to be good decisions than those based on whim. Your business is too important to risk the consequences of a lot of hasty decisions. An idea that still seems sound after you sleep on it is probably a good idea.

Remember the old adages 'More haste less speed' and 'Look before you leap'? They apply to business.

- **Follow your strengths and interests.** They will sustain your enthusiasm. If you like selling but hate bookkeeping, hire a bookkeeper so you can do what you like doing. After all, one reason for going into business is to be able to exercise your favourite skills and interests. Listen to yourself (never easy, but always necessary) and be honest. If you don't like being in charge, or being responsible, or taking risks, don't try to start a business.

- **Don't be too proud to give up.** If your idea doesn't feel right, don't press on just because you don't want to give up. You may be able to modify the start-up plan, or switch to another business, or overcome whatever doesn't feel right. That's fine. There's a big difference between being persistent and being pigheaded. If the idea continues to raise more doubts and worries, it may not be the right idea for you, or the right time to pursue it. Be prepared to abandon your business idea if the facts tell you it makes sense to do so. Part of the value of planning is that it reveals warning signals.

Be prepared to abandon your business idea if the facts tell you it makes sense to do so.

There are no ready charted routes to a successful start-up. There are no short cuts either. However, if you pay attention to your personal goals and desires, make sure your business goals reflect them, and proceed carefully, you will greatly increase your chances of success.

CHAPTER 2

ONE YEAR BEFORE START-UP

To provide the best launch for your business, start to keep track of your thoughts a year or so before start-up. A three-ring looseleaf notebook is a good format, since you will want to rethink some of your ideas over the next few months, make changes and keep a note of the way these changes are made. Don't trust your memory. As a Chinese proverb puts it, the finest memory is not as firm as faded ink.

The finest memory is not as firm as faded ink.

The point of this exercise is to ask yourself questions, write down your answers and move on. The process is self-correcting – that is, you will change your answers as you go along. Starting a business is such an intriguing activity that this process is a lot of fun. Your ideas change, you change and your business will ultimately be the better for it.

Refine your ideas

You already have a pretty clear idea of what your business will be. Use the next six months to clarify this picture, make it sharper and better defined, test your assumptions and improve your business management skills.

Your choice of what kind of business to start is influenced by any number of factors. Some of the more obvious ones include your background, education and work experience. Less obvious are your answers to questions such as: Whom do you want for customers and clients? What type of technology do you want to be involved in? How hard do you want to work? How much money do you want/need to earn? What are your long-term goals?

Note that at this point you can choose what business to go into. Once you have invested substantial cash and effort, your choices will be much narrower, so from the outset you should try to make sure that the business you want to start is indeed the right one for you. The 'I am going to get rich quick by doing something I don't like doing' attitude leads to failure. Choosing to start a business that reflects your interests and personal goals, on the other hand, is far more rewarding.

Look at all kinds of businesses. If you are interested in opening a shop, check out lots of different shops selling lots of different products. All will have something of value for you. If the hospitality industry intrigues you, look into restaurants, guesthouses, bed-and-breakfast places and so on. If you plan to manufacture something, find and look at as many similar manufacturing businesses as you can. The wider the range of your search, the better your final choice will be, and the more information you will acquire.

Decide what business you want to start

Weigh your choice against your resources, experience and expectations

Successful start-ups depend on a good balance of resources and owner experience. Ask yourself these kinds of question and jot down your answers:

- **How much money can I invest?** Businesses, especially during the start-up period, run on cash. Most small businesses are started with a combination of savings and 'house money' (a shorthand term for savings, inheritances, investments from friends and relations, cash value of life insurance policies and equity in a residence or other assets), augmented by trade credit and, in some but not all cases, bank debt and outside investment. The cash you invest becomes permanent capital in the business. The amount required will vary from one business to the next and will depend to some extent on your degree of experience in the business. Extensive experience can sometimes lower the need for direct capital investment; little

Extensive experience can sometimes lower the need for direct capital investment.

19

experience requires greater capital to provide a margin for the inevitable errors made during start-up.

- **Can (and should) I attract other investors?** Even if you have enough cash to avoid involving other investors, don't automatically go it alone. You may want other investors in order to get a strong management team, acquire specific skills or otherwise bolster your company's chances of success. Against this, investors want some degree of control, and while this is negotiable to some degree, it isn't always in your best interest to involve these outsiders.

You will want to hire people with the specific skills you lack in order to concentrate on doing what you do best.

- **What do I do well?** Most of us tend to be good at only a few of the tasks that running a business requires. For example, you might be strong on sales and weak on finance, or terrific at managing people but hopeless at marketing. Knowing your strengths and weaknesses helps you to balance your business better. You will want to hire people with the specific skills you lack (or rent their skills on an ad hoc basis) in order to concentrate on doing what you do best.

- **What do I like doing?** One of the best tips to what you do best is to look at what you like doing. What have you enjoyed doing in the past? Do you like to initiate actions, or do you prefer to follow a clear set of directions? Do you prefer to do things yourself, or do you like to delegate and control? One of the best things about your own business is that you can often set it up to allow you to do what you like doing most – and minimise the time spent doing things you loathe. That doesn't mean that you won't have to do a lot of things that aren't fun. Wait until you have to dismiss an employee (a task you can't delegate). But, on balance, you will have more control over how you spend your time and effort than you would working for somebody else.

The key concept here is that you will strive harder, longer and with more enjoyment at work that interests you. Work that you don't like will, over time, be done grudgingly and perhaps less thoroughly than it should be. The ultimate cost to your business will be higher than if you had known in the first place what you didn't like doing and paid someone else to do those tasks.

- **What would I like to be doing five years from now?** A five-year horizon is useful as a defining tool. In five years you might want to open another shop, manage a much larger practice, devote your time to research, or whatever. Use the five-year test to help yourself to understand what you like doing. If you're working towards a goal (not necessarily financial, though financial goals are important, too), the day-to-day frustrations of small-business life are easier to handle. The five-year horizon also helps you to define some benchmarks and a plan for reaching them. Maybe you want to be able to spend more time with your family, do community work or some other non-business activity. That's fine: the ability to pursue such goals through building your own business is one of the most potent and satisfying motivators imaginable. Purely business goals ('make a million pounds and retire at the age of 40') tend to be poor motivators, and in the long run unsatisfying. So you make a million. What then? Make two million? Ten? I bet you won't retire. Building a business is too much fun.

- **What kind of return do I want?** Some businesses are inherently limited in potential, while others have the possibility for unlimited growth. Much of the potential depends on you. One young woman turned a cake shop (usually local and limited) into a very large enterprise. A highly successful ice cream emporium began in a garage. The business ideas (make a better cake, make tastier ice cream) could have led, in different hands, to dwarfed businesses.

- **Some businesses are more profitable than others.** A motorcycle repairer, discouraged because he wasn't making much money, left to return to work for a company after he found that his business was in the top 10 per cent of all motorcycle repair shops in terms both of absolute profit and percentage of sales turned to profit. No matter how well he ran his business, he wouldn't achieve his income goals. On the other hand, take convenience stores, the prototype family business. In the right hands, the 7-Eleven chain grew big enough to swallow Gulf Oil. Without a hiccup.

Don't choose a business because you think it will make you rich if you don't like that business.

Choose a business you like, and then make it grow. Don't choose a business because you think it will make you rich if you don't like that business.

Use 'constructive daydreaming' to set business goals that are consistent with your personal goals

Daydreams play an interesting and important role in starting a business. First, the initial idea to start a business often comes in the form of a daydream: What if I had started Apple? What would it be like to run that business? I know I could improve on this business – here's what I'd do.

Second, constructive daydreaming is an excellent technique for trying out the 'fit' between business and personal goals. The aim here is to form a sketch of your business which can be filled in as you go along. Imagine going to the office every day. What are you doing? How does it feel? What do you do when you aren't at the office? And so on. Your business is going to be an extension of your own personality no matter how hard you try to make it something else, so it makes good sense to look ahead. If the picture doesn't feel right, the chances are that there is a disparity between what you want to do and what the business, as you project it, makes you do. You'll have plenty of compromises to make without setting the stage for long-term, self-defeating behaviour. Running a business to achieve goals you don't like is stupid. Projecting the future doesn't determine the future, but it does help you to twist the odds in your favour.

Assess the impact on your family and personal life

Starting a business affects every facet of your life. There are always loose ends to tie up, work to do and bills to pay. The result is that your family and social life will suffer. While this is usually a problem only until the business settles into a routine, it is serious enough to cause many enterprises to fail. A supportive family and understanding friends go a long way towards making your business a success.

Make sure you consider how your new venture will affect your:

- **Income.** Unless you are able to retain your full-time job and start your business as a part-time enterprise, your income will suffer. Start-up businesses don't usually provide a decent salary to the owner right away. If you can, save some money to plug this gap. A second income (a supportive spouse, in many cases) can also make a big difference.

- **Hours.** Start-ups devour time. In the first few months of a business, when everything is new and short cuts haven't been discovered, you'll literally live your business. You'll think about it all the time, whether at the office or not. Your time will not be your own – one of the biggest problems newcomers to small business ownership face is that they can't forget the business at 5 o'clock and go home. They take the business with them. So will you.

- **Support level.** Wholehearted support from family and friends helps you avoid burnout. People who take an intelligent interest in your business can provide you with objective advice and criticism. To get this kind of support, keep them informed from the start. Don't keep everything to yourself. If you are worried, tell them. If you are uncertain, tell them.

The loneliness that goes with small business ownership is self-induced. Somehow the myth of the rugged individual who never shows the least sign of doubt or fear has become mixed up with being the owner. Don't believe the myth. Your family and friends have a sizeable emotional investment in you and your business. Let them help, and they will. Give them a return on their investment and all of you benefit. They will understand the demands of your business better, and this in turn defuses their concerns about the amount of time, effort and worry you put into your start up.

> The myth of the rugged individual who never shows the least sign of doubt or fear has become mixed up with being the owner.

- **Commitment to family, community and leisure activities.** Many entrepreneurs find that the lack of time for family, community and leisure activities (hobbies, sports, reading, etc) is the highest price they pay for business ownership. During the start-up period this price is reasonable. Later, when the business is actually running, it becomes a major cause of burnout. At this point, make sure you have a clear picture of what your commitments will be, how long they will take to fulfil, and what sacrifices (if any) you will have to make.

Some other considerations you should bear in mind:

- Some businesses are more limiting than others. A retail or hospitality business demands that the owner should be there all the time. The hours are long, the rewards high – but it may not be a good choice for a person who places a premium on family or community activities.

Don't expect to lose yourself in your start up and magically come out of it with a better marriage.

- A shaky marriage or other relationship is never improved by starting a business (or buying one). Don't expect to lose yourself in your start-up and magically come out of it with a better marriage.

- Starting your business should be a positive and exciting experience. Negative motivations don't last; positive motivations do, which is why it is so important that you place your personal goals ahead of your business goals. Your business should serve your goals.

Begin your research

Information sources come in two varieties: 'hot' and 'cool'. You will need both kinds. 'Hot' information is interpersonal, interactive and provides immediate feedback; 'cool' information sources are more passive, and for many entrepreneurs less fun. Reading, observing and attending lectures are good examples of cool information. Although these activities are not too interactive, they have high information value for the time invested.

Get hot information

Work in management in your chosen line of business. While this is not always a possible option, you can't beat it for value. You will learn the tricks of the trade, the jargon, and when and where problems tend to crop up. You get to know suppliers, customers and how to keep the customers happy. And you get paid while doing so. Almost as good as this is working in a non-management position. While your experience won't be as broad, it will be direct and immediately valuable.

Talk to people in your proposed line of business. Ask current and former owners a lot of questions: What's different about your business? What's good or bad about it? How do you see the future? What kinds of problem do you encounter? What are normal trade terms?

Find out the names of experts and other helpful hot information sources. If you draw up a list of questions, you can make sure that you don't impose on their time, and you enhance the value of the information you receive. Keep notes: hot information melts away if you don't write it down.

Some other hot information sources are:

- **Businesses in non-competitive locations.** Take a trip and search out business owners. Tell them what you're up to and point out that you won't be competing. The magic words 'I've got a problem and I think you can help me' open many doors.

- **Competitors.** Quite often, competitors are willing to talk to you. Try them.

- **Attend trade fairs.** Don't miss this one. Trade fairs are a great source of hot information. Many of the suppliers and consultants to the industry will be there as well as the leading businesses. Almost every industry has a trade fair, and it's non-stop shopping for hot information sources.

- **Trade association executives and editors, consultants to the industry, financers of industry (include local bank managers), and career counsellors in the industry.** Anyone with direct connections to the industry will often have useful insights. Make sure you get in touch with these people.

- Start with the *Small Firms Service*. You can make contact by dialling the operator on 100 and asking for Freefone Enterprise. This service is provided by the Department of Employment and has branches in certain major towns of England and Wales. It is staffed by experts in the fields of employment legislation, patents, exports etc. There are also advisers with experience in different types of business. The client is entitled to three free counselling sessions with the Small Firms Counsellor. After that, the fee is £30 a day.

- In many areas where the Small Firms Service does not operate, it has been absorbed by the new Training and Enterprise Councils (TECs). 80 are in the course of being set up

   In Scotland the service is provided by the *Scottish Development Agency* and the *Highlands and Islands Development Board*; in Wales by the *Welsh Development Agency* and *Enterprise Mid-Wales*; and in Northern Ireland by the *Local Enterprise Development Unit* in Belfast.

- The Rural Development Commission. Until recently known as the Council for Small Industries in Rural Areas, the RDC operates in English towns with a population of under 10,000. It offers a range of services to stimulate industry and employment, such as advice on business management, eg marketing and bookkeeping. It runs a wide range of courses both in business management and individual crafts. Its financial service has a loan service and a tie-up with four major banks.

- Local Development Boards. These government agencies are responsible for developing their areas. They give advice, training, loans and grants to enterprises which will create jobs.

- Tourist boards offer help, advice and financial support for tourism projects, including leisure amenities. They can indicate whether particular schemes would qualify for assistance.

- Enterprise agencies. Each agency (there are over 500 of them, at least 20 in London alone) is independent and funded by local industry. They exist to encourage the formation and good management of commercially viable small businesses. The managers, usually people with many years of business experience, offer counselling on business proposals for new start-ups and help to prepare the business plan. All services are free.

- **Your local chamber of commerce.** Chambers of commerce act as clearing houses for small business schemes and information sources. They will give you information, whether you are a member or not. Addresses of organisations mentioned in this chapter are given in the Appendix on page 136.

Get cool information
Books, lectures and other less social activities tend to be more solitary and analytic than hot information sources, but don't ignore their value.

Start with your local librarian. He or she will help you to organise and plan your research. If you have access to a business library, pay it a visit and ask for help. Your research should include:

- Trade publications, especially periodicals
- Trade association publications
- Government publications, including the wide range of low-cost or

free publications available through the Small Firms Service.
- Check the Resources listed in the Appendix (page 136).

Organise the information you gather in a clip file and invest in some manila folders, paper and pencils. Take notes on those articles or books you can't clip to your file. The database you build over a few weeks saves you months of work later on. A lot of basic demographic and market research can be gleaned from magazines and journals. Once more, ask your librarian for help.

Build your skills by taking formal management courses

Formal management courses are a fast way of learning if you've had little management experience. Remember, there is no prize for re-inventing standard management practices which have evolved over years through the painstaking efforts of millions of intelligent people.

Formal management courses are a fast way of learning if you've had little management experience.

- Courses are run at colleges throughout the country, as well as many business schools and universities. Phone your nearest college of further education to find out what is on offer. The courses last from a few days to a few weeks. The costs are variable depending on the amount of sponsorship. Distance learning is possible through the Open University and the Rapid Results College.

- Pickup (professional, industrial and commercial updating) programmes are operated in colleges, polytechnics and universities. The national centre for information is the Adult Training Promotions Unit, Department of Education and Science.

- Local Enterprise Agencies often have a training team who organise local programmes. There are hundreds of these throughout the country and a list is published by Business in the Community (see page 136).

- The Industry Training Boards should be contacted for information on local courses for new and existing entrepreneurs. There are seven ITBs, covering the following areas, as well as the Agricultural Training Board.

Clothing and Allied Products
Construction

Engineering
Hotel and Catering
Offshore Petroleum
Plastics Processing
Road Transport

- The larger chambers of commerce often run series of lectures on specific subjects. Your local chamber will be able to supply details.

- Trade and professional associations will be a source of information.

- The British Institute of Management keeps a register of business training courses.

Use the year before starting your business to visualise and flesh out a picture of your business, including its impact on your personal life. Take skill-building courses and conduct basic research to increase the odds in your favour. This includes both interactive and solitary research. Find out about and make use of the government schemes that have been established to help you successfully start your own business. And don't fail to take your local librarian out to lunch: his or her skills are highly professional, seldom called upon by business owners, and extraordinarily helpful to you in this research phase of your start-up.

Action Plan

Objective	Action/Strategy	Target date	Person responsible	Results/Comments
Choose the right business for you	Start to use notebook and clip files (immediate, ongoing)			
	List businesses that appeal to you (for two weeks)			
	Weigh choices against your experience (30 days)			
	Use constructive daydreaming (ongoing)			
	Weigh impact on personal and family goals (30–60 days)			
Test your assumptions	Begin research (immediate)			
	Visit businesses that interest you (10 days)			
	Research in your library (10 days)			
	Look up trade publications (within 60 days)			
	Discuss idea with friends, family (ongoing)			
	Get basic Small Firms Service literature (30–60 days)			
Improve your business management skills	Take Management Audit in Appendix, page 123 (within 30 days)			
	Visit or talk to Small Firms Service (within 30 days)			
	Take a pre-business seminar (within 30 days)			
	Look into local business schemes			

◄ CHAPTER 3 ►

SIX MONTHS BEFORE START-UP

Decide the focus of your business

The key start-up question is: What business are you really in? Your answer will influence all your business plans and affect your perception of your markets. This in turn will determine what kind of research will be of most benefit to you, what groups to join or ally yourself to, and (for professional service, retail and hospitality businesses) where to locate your business.

The immediate impulse is to say, 'I'm in the computer business', or, 'I sell display units to department stores'. These are the beginnings of answers, built on products or markets. The aim is to define what business you are in, what you sell and to whom, and what makes your business different – all in 25 words or less. You will use the resulting mission statement or company motto to keep your enterprise focused on its primary business. One of the biggest pitfalls for new businesses is to be unclear about the thrust of the business. As a result, efforts are scattered and fragmentary, many expensive and distracting false starts are made, and all too often the fledgling business is crippled.

The aim is to define what business you are in, what you sell and to whom, and what makes your business different.

A good mission statement will help to decide what you should do. As an example, a business publisher's mission statement might be: 'To provide useful, applicable business management tools to small business owners and advisers and organisations serving small business owners.' This defines what is offered ('useful, applicable management tools', which include books and other publications now, and cassettes and other media for use in the future); it determines the market, which limits expensive over-advertising; and it sets up a distinctive characteristic of the product line: the tools must be useful and applicable.

Start with your market

To whom will you be selling? Always place the customer (actual or prospective) at the centre of your plans. If you don't have customers, you don't have a business.

One of the biggest benefits of a start-up is that you have some latitude in determining who your customers will be. All things being equal, it's better to deal with people you like, respect and are comfortable with than with people you dislike, look down on or are uncomfortable with. Your realistic target markets need what you plan to sell, are accessible to you (through advertising and other promotional means as well as through your location and methods of distribution) and have some reason to buy from you rather than from your competitors. They are also big enough and rich enough to make your venture a profitable one. You should know a lot about your markets, which is a function of your experience and familiarity with them.

One of the biggest benefits of a start-up is that you have some latitude in determining who your customers will be.

Bear in mind that all buying decisions are made by individuals, and are ultimately subjective. For this reason alone, your chances of success are enhanced by your familiarity with the people in your target markets. If you don't know them, make sure you know somebody who does. Few things are less rewarding and more costly than selling into markets you know little or nothing about.

Definition
Markets are those persons or organisations who will be your customers, while target markets are those persons or organisations most likely to become your customers. Target markets are small and tightly defined. A common start-up error is to assume that everyone is a prospective customer. Everyone is not. Your markets are limited by geography, age, education, income and other demographic factors, competition, your skill at promoting and advertising your business, and dozens of other factors. And even your target markets will have different sub-groups of greater or lesser value to you. Think of a bull's eye (most valuable

31

prospects) versus outer rings (less valuable prospects) on an archery board. You want to concentrate on the bull's eye and not squander your efforts and resources trying to reach less likely prospects.

Choose your products and/or services

Ideally your goods and services will be chosen with your prospective customers (target markets) in mind. What can you offer your markets that they are ready and eager to buy? Start-ups which try to educate their markets to something brand new and different are rarely successful. Leave education to large, established businesses.

Give serious consideration to these questions:

- What are the products or services you plan to sell?
- How will your target markets find out about you?
- Why would your target markets buy these goods or services?
- When will they buy them? Sporadically (legal advice, jewellery, travel), or weekly (groceries), annually (insurance), seasonally (sporting goods)?
- How will they pay: cash or credit? Purchase in large or small lots?
- What price range are you going to offer?
- Where are they going to find or use your product or service?

Every decision you make in your business should include consideration of your markets.

Notice that these questions all have marketing components. Every decision you make in your business should include consideration of your markets. If you forget your customers, your customers will forget you – fast. And remember that without customers, you don't have a business.

What makes your business different?

What will set you apart from your competitors?

Differentiation (or positioning) is arguably the most important small business marketing strategy. Your aim is to locate a market niche, a market large enough to be profitable, small enough to defend against other businesses, and suited to your resources, interests and abilities.

Some differentiating ideas will fit your start-up; others won't. You want to decide well ahead how you wish to position your business so you can influence the perceptions of your market. If you plan to sell on quality, you will go one way; if you decide to differentiate your business on grounds of convenience, price or durability, you have other options. You cannot follow all of them without hopelessly blurring your image.

Here are some ways businesses differentiate their products and services. Feel free to add to this list:

- Quality
- Service
- Perceived value
- Convenience
- Reliability
- Price
- Familiarity
- Local son or daughter
- Warranty
- Financing options
- Product range —
- Specialisation
- Credentials
- Method of production
- Accessibility of purchase

As you get more familiar with your product or service, markets and competition, you will begin to see other ways of differentiating your business. The important thing is to be careful and consistent. The image your business projects when it starts will be very hard to change later, if it can be changed at all.

> **The image your business projects when it starts will be very hard to change later, if it can be changed at all.**

Start writing your business plan

A business plan (see Figure 3.1) is a short written document that serves as a guide to your future, provides direction and focus, and helps you model your business and avoid problems. As noted in Chapter 2, avail yourself of business seminars to get started on your plan. Also get a copy of *The Business Plan Workbook*, which is described in the Appendix on page 145.

Your business plan helps you to define your financing needs with some accuracy. More importantly, it makes running your business much easier.

Figure 3.1 *Outline of a business plan*

- Cover: Name of business, names of directors/partners, address and phone number
- Statement of Purpose
- Table of Contents

Section 1: The Business
  A. Description of business
  B. Product/service
  C. Market
  D. Location of business
  E. Competition
  F. Management
  G. Personnel
  H. Application and expected effect of loan (if needed)
  I. Summary

Section 2: Financial data
  A. Sources and applications of funds
  B. Capital equipment list
  C. Balance sheet
  D. Break-even analysis
  E. Income projections (profit and loss statements)
    1. Three-year summary
    2. Detail by month for first year
    3. Detail by quarter for second and third years
    4. Explanatory notes
  F. Cash flow projection
    1. Detail by month for first year
    2. Detail by quarter for second and third years
    3. Explanatory notes
  G. Deviation analysis
  H. Historical financial reports for existing business
    1. Balance sheets for past three years
    2. Income statements for past three years
    3. Tax returns

Section 3: Supporting documents
Personal CVs, personal balance sheets, cost of living budget, credit reports, letters of reference, job descriptions, letters of intent, copies of leases, contracts, legal documents and anything else relevant to the plan.

Refine your initial mission statement or company motto

What business are you going to be in? Keep working at your answers; it should change as your research progresses. Remember that your aim is to find ways of making your business stand out from others, including both direct and indirect competitors.

List your strongest competition

Competition is a fact of business life. If you have no competitors, you probably don't have a viable business idea, or haven't come to grips with what business you are really in. Theodore Levitt, in a classic essay entitled 'Marketing Myopia', noted that some years ago Hollywood decided that it was in the business of making films, and that television was no competition. After losing billions of dollars of business to this newer medium, Hollywood finally realised that it was in the entertainment business, not just films, and began to compete successfully.

All businesses have competition. List your five closest direct competitors and begin to collect information on them. Cut out copies of their advertisements, note down your observations on them, pay them visits as a customer.

You will partially define your business by your competition. Most businesses operate within fairly tight parameters: all grocers' shops carry more or less the same items; one hardware shop is very much like another; solicitors are interchangeable. Within these limits of product, service and distribution, there are plenty of ways to set yourself apart. A grocer's shop might offer a particularly wide range of delicatessen or frozen goods; a hardware shop might have a good stock of car parts; a solicitor might specialise.

You will partially define your business by your competition.

The better you know your competition, the better able you will be to compete. Start with the most direct competitors, but keep an eye out for indirect competition – those businesses that are not obvious competitors. For example, retail outlets have to contend with mail order competition; and some mail order firms have begun to open retail outlets in prime locations. If you can spot these trends early, you can compete.

Your competitor list will grow. Start it early, add to it as needed, and be prepared to receive disproportionate benefits from your research.

Prepare your personal financial statement

A cost of living budget form is provided in the Appendix on page 128; it helps you to get a grip on what your basic income needs add up to. Make sure to add 30 per cent to this figure, since underestimating income needs is a major problem for new business owners. If your income doesn't meet your basic needs, worry and panic set in. If you take out too much, you can strangle your cash flow. Setting a realistic balance is extremely important.

When you work out your personal financial statements and cost of living budget, get your spouse (or partner or other family supporters) to go over it with you. The fewer surprises you spring on them, the more supportive they'll be when you need them.

Define your target markets

Defining target markets is another ongoing project. Don't do it once and expect to enjoy success. Your markets change. People move. Tastes change. Competition increases, especially in profitable markets. Products and services change, and what sold yesterday won't necessarily sell today.

Eventually, you will redefine your markets almost unconsciously. However, that takes experience, and to offset a lack of experience, be prepared to go through a lot of spadework.

Interview prospective customers

You can't beat prospective customers as a source of hot information.

You can't beat prospective customers as a source of hot information. Ask yourself who might buy your goods and services, then interview them. Your Training and Enterprise Council or Small Firms Service advisers will help you to determine your best markets. Use them. They can also help with surveys and basic market research. (See 'Begin your research' on page 24.)

People like to express their opinions. You must listen to them, as this information will help you to define what your business will be. People buy what they want to buy, which is not necessarily what you plan to sell.

Visit similar businesses

Businesses like yours are another important source of information. Visit as many as you can. To whom are they selling? How do they sell? How do they differentiate themselves?

This kind of research is far superior to armchair research for one major reason: it is up to date. By the time you have read an article or book, the information is dated. That doesn't mean that it's valueless – but it does mean that you, as an astute entrepreneur, will want to make sure that your information is still valid.

Important questions your research should cover
Whether you're interviewing prospective accountants, meeting new colleagues at a chamber of commerce function, or talking to people from your trade association, be sure to ask:

- How is business in this area – is it growing? Stable?
- What is the economic outlook for this industry?
- How many businesses like mine can this region support?
- What questions should someone in my position be asking?

Research business and trade organisations

Trade and business organisations are another source of valuable information. There are hundreds in the United Kingdom, so the odds are that you'll be able to find one that fits the kind of business you plan to start.

This is cool information at its most efficient, because trade associations are the best single source of specific industry information available. They have to be: their mission is to provide up-to-date, specific information to their members.

Most trade associations have regional (and sometimes local) branches. Pay yours a visit. Most of them also have publications for their members and the information you get is worth the price of membership. It is targeted to your business, delivered to you with the post, links you to businesses similar to yours and provides a forum for asking questions. And you can always phone the editor and ask more detailed questions. Editors are expected to spot trends and problems and to answer questions.

Business associations are less well defined but nonetheless valuable as a way of meeting other business owners and participating in educational activities.

Ask your librarian for help

Ask your nearest business librarian to help you find trade information on your business. He or she will steer you to the CBD *Directory of British Associations* and other listings.

Also, ask him or her:

- What your SIC (Standard Industrial Classification) Code number is – all government data is listed by SIC number
- About business census data
- What current general business journals you should read
- About trade publications
- For books specific to your industry
- What your library can get hold of for you through inter-library loans.

Get in touch with your chamber of commerce

Chambers of commerce provide local information, business education schemes, mailing lists and a chance to rub elbows with other business owners.

Join your chamber of commerce. Chambers of commerce provide local information, business education schemes, mailing lists and a chance to rub elbows with other business owners. The last may be the most important, because when you have started your business, you'll have questions that are best answered by people who have successfully answered the same questions.

Local business groups other than the chamber, such as certain professional associations, are worth looking into, but are secondary in importance. You won't have a lot of time for these associations when you are in business, though during the pre-start-up period they can provide helpful insights and contacts.

Look in your daily paper for listings of local business organisations. You can often find out what's available by contacting the business editor; alternatively, a few minutes spent looking over the business pages will give you names and addresses of groups that might appeal to you.

Seek the best location

Your business location should be chosen with great care. Investing time in choosing a good location well ahead of start-up pays off handsomely.

For some kinds of businesses (retail and hospitality in particular), location is all-important. For other businesses (craft, small manufacturing, some services), location is less vital. However, making a decision on cost concerns alone is still risky. Location and image are so tightly intertwined that the wrong location can undermine an otherwise sound business.

A shopfront is vital to a retail business, partly because it is the most direct channel of distribution between shop and customer. If you provide a service, you must also think in terms of distribution channels. How will you keep your prospects alert to your business existence? Where will you deliver the service – your place or theirs? If you are a manufacturer (including crafts), how will you get the products from your site to the retailers or intermediaries who take your products to the consumer? Line up your distribution channels early, and include distribution considerations in your search for the right location for your business.

Include distribution considerations in your search for the right location for your business.

Talk to estate agents and banks

Before settling on a location, consult the people who can help you to make a wise choice. Estate agents are knowledgeable about markets for commercial property, but talk to more than one and don't rely on them alone. Talk to your bank manager and other advisers. Banks provide another viewpoint for evaluating commercial locations and are often aware of trends earlier than other people.

Don't jump at the first good site. Choose from a variety of locations, and take your time. If you decide to rent, remember that leases are negotiable. They are also hard to get out of, so be sure to get legal advice before you sign.

Consider image, clientele and business aims relative to your business's location

One important set of questions to do with choosing a location revolves around the image you wish your business to project. Since money spent on space is a fixed cost – one that you have to pay every month no matter how sales are – this is no trivial matter.

- How do you want your target markets to perceive your business?
- Is there a shopping precinct or business development area or professional office park where your business should be located?
- Will you depend on passing trade?
- Is the location consistent with the image you want to project? A discount store in a luxury location or a luxury goods shop in a downmarket area would be inappropriate.
- Where are your competitors situated? Why did they choose the location?
- What help does your trade association offer with site selection?
- Check with your TEC or small business advisers. What do they recommend?
- What is the rent versus advertising cost ratio? Low rent and high advertising costs tend to go together.
- If location is not very important to your business, you still have to ask how your customers will find you, what the impact of the location will be on your image, and how you will justify your choice. For example, consultants often use a fancy address to impress prospective clients, even if actual meetings take place at the client's place of business. A street address inspires more confidence than a post office box number, which has implications of here today, gone tomorrow.

Choice of location is a major concern. Take your time. For now, just look round and ask questions. You can make your choice later.

Action Plan

Objective	Action/Strategy	Target date	Person responsible	Results/Comments
Determine what business you'll be in	Write mission statement (immediate) – Know what products/services you'll offer			
	List strongest competitors (within 30 days)			
	Visit businesses similar to yours			
	Test statement for clarity (within 30 days)			
	Start writing your business plan			
	Revise mission statement			
Prepare personal financial statements				
Decide who your customers should be	Interview prospective customers (ongoing)			
	Determine competitors' target markets (within 30 days)			
	Prepare initial product/service benefit list (30–60 days)			
	Talk to trade sources, advisers (ongoing)			
Know your industry thoroughly	Involve library in research (ongoing)			
	Involve Small Firms Service or other counsellors (ongoing)			
	Keep a notebook, clip files (ongoing)			
Find the best location for your business	Talk to estate agents, bank managers, chamber of commerce (30 days)			
	Research trade association's site suggestions (30 days)			
	Check locations for fit with image, clientele (60 days)			

◀ CHAPTER 4 ▶

FOUR MONTHS BEFORE START-UP

Four months before opening, concentrate on making the picture developed over the past six months more precise. This helps you to set the stage for figures to enter the picture. Avoid the fun-with-numbers approach whereby the financial goals are set first, then the vision and assumptions moulded to fit those goals. If the financial model you will build in Chapter 5 is to be useful to you, it must flow from your vision and assumptions. You will have plenty of time to make adjustments over the next four months, so this does not tie you to just one set of ideas.

You can now begin to address several major problems. Among these are naming your business, choosing the location for your business and deciding on your professional advisers. Once you know what your business will be, and who are most likely to be your solicitor, accountant and bank manager, you can get answers to a still more specific set of questions, such as whether or not to form a company, what bookkeeping and accounting systems make sense for your business, and what key skills and information your business will still need.

Name your business

The name you choose will fix your business in people's minds, affect the image you project, and have a major impact on your success.

Naming your business is a pleasant task. It makes it easier to visualise the business, and somehow makes the entire start-up process feel more real.

It is also an important task: the name you choose will fix your business in people's minds, affect the image you project and have a major impact on your success. Some guidelines may help you to think through the naming process. These are not intended to prevent you from being creative or whimsical (anyone who named his business 'Upstart Publishing Company, Inc' is disqualified from offering this kind of advice!), but they are intended to help you avoid the unintended consequences of a hastily chosen name.

Naming your business is an important marketing decision. Bear in mind that one major marketing rule is to minimise customer (and prospect) discontent.

- **Keep the name straightforward and descriptive.** The name you pick should tell people what your business is about, not baffle them. 'Jack's Joke Shop' is straightforward. But what's an 'EXXON'? A 'Primerica'? To answer these questions, these companies spend millions of dollars every year.

The name you pick should tell people what your business is about.

- **Make the name distinctive, if possible.** You still want to stand out from the crowd. 'Finestkind Seafoods' is clear and direct.

- **Avoid humour.** What you think is funny your markets may not. Humour is a dangerous marketing tool at best.

- **Avoid grandiose descriptions.** 'Supreme', 'Universal', and so forth have been overworked to the point where they are meaningless.

- **Don't pick the first name that comes to you.** Make a list. Ask your friends. Look in the Yellow Pages, not just in your area but in other places. (If in doubt, don't use a famous name. Ask your solicitor.)

- **Try your business name out on people who don't know you and your business idea.** They may give you positive feedback – or constructive criticism. Run it through your advertising agency or marketing advisers. It's easy to change the name now. It won't be once you develop a logo, stationery, business cards, signs and put your phone and fax numbers in the Yellow Pages.

- **Some names carry an embargo** unless you have previously obtained approval of the Secretary of State for Trade and Industry.

A full list is available from The Registrar of Companies in Cardiff. Some examples are:

International	Association
British	Society
European	Institute
Authority	Group
Board	Foundation
Council	Trust

In addition, some words or expressions in business names need permission from an official body as well as the Secretary of State. They include:

Royal	Health Centre	Charity
Dental	Nursing Home	University

If in doubt, take legal advice.

Select your location

You've thought about where your business should be located – now it's time to make your selection. Four months before opening should be enough time to arrange for all the improvements and changes you want to make, yet not too long a time to pay rent before making money. If you are setting up a home-based business, plan on spending about the same length of time establishing a suitable office in your home.

Rent = Space Cost + Advertising

As a rule, it is safer to spend more on location and less on advertising than vice versa. Advertising always carries an element of risk. If your target market likes to shop at middle-of-the-range stores, putting your store in the same range will pay off. Choose your location based on your target market's buying habits, patterns and expectations.

You will pay a premium for some locations – but if you try another one, the saving won't make up for the wrong location. Have you ever noticed how certain kinds of business such as fast food restaurants, car dealers, department stores and DIY stores flock together? There's a good reason for it. If you know where the car dealers are, you can shop around. Competition increases everyone's business. An isolated dealer (or fast food restaurant or jewellery shop) will slowly but surely fade.

Realise that cheapest is not always least expensive

Space cost is a combination of rent or mortgage payment, utilities, leasehold improvements, general maintenance, security, insurance and all costs relating to having a place to conduct your business. A premium rent may be less expensive once you tot up the bills than an apparently less expensive one.

Choosing a location because the rent is cheap is risky. Your location speaks loudly to your customers, and if it says the wrong thing you will lose sales. Your choice of location, like your choice of a business name, is very hard to change once you've committed yourself to it. Choose carefully, with your customers' and prospects' needs and habits in mind, and choose wisely. After all, it's more important for your customers to approve of your location than for you to approve of it.

Choosing a location because the rent is cheap is risky.

Set up a network

Now that you've had time to research the organisations which might be useful, join them. As owner of a local start-up business, you should join your chamber of commerce and be an active member; this is an important part of your marketing effort. The benefits outweigh the costs: you will find that as a new member with a new business you will receive a lot of business (and publicity) that would not otherwise have come your way.

Trade associations are another matter. You may want to economise by subscribing to trade journals (or go to the library and see if they subscribe to them) and not joining as a fully-fledged member until you see the benefits.

Select outside advisers

The correlation between using outside advisers and success in business is so high that only the most hell-bent-on-failure individualists try to go it alone. 'Using' means asking for advice and following it. Soliciting advice from experts and then not following it is silly.

The correlation between using outside advisers and success in business is high.

There are two important kinds of adviser you should try to recruit. The first includes your professional advisers; the second is informal advisers, other business owners and friends. Running a business is a notoriously lonely affair, so recruiting this second group is important. Usually, all you have to do is to ask them for help and keep them informed. Professional advisers, on the other hand, have to be paid one way or another.

Choose and meet your:

- solicitor
- accountant
- bank manager
- insurance broker
- bookkeeper (optional)
- advertising agent (optional)
- Small Firms Service or TEC adviser
- business consultants

You need a competent solicitor, accountant, insurance broker, and bank manager. Shop around for these professionals. Pick the ones you are most comfortable with. You'll have plenty to do without attempting to be your own solicitor and accountant (anyway, only fools have themselves for clients).

If your start-up involves complicated record keeping, talk to your accountant. He or she will set up (and even maintain) a bookkeeping system that's appropriate for your business.

You don't have the same level of need for an advertising agency. However, the cost of poor advertising and promotion is extravagant. Putting out the wrong message and creating the wrong image for your business immediately costs money, but the opportunity cost of lost sales is tremendous. Once your advertising and marketing efforts are fairly routine you can economise (though if you have capable advisers you won't want to), but to make sure that you start out on the right foot, hire experts. Don't try to learn advertising and promotion techniques on the job.

Consultants (including the free or low-cost ones already mentioned) serve a variety of functions. The most important come from their depth of experience. They can save you time, money and misspent effort. For example, a marketing consultant with ten years' experience in your particular industry will have put together scores of marketing plans, monitoring their progress and made constant improvements. That experience, put to use for your start up, can make all the difference. True, consultants cost a lot, but you are buying their training and experience, not just their current time. If you can afford to invest in a marketing consultant at the outset, it's a wise move. Otherwise, talk to Small Firms Service personnel and try to find the person with the best feeling for your business and its marketing problems.

If you can afford to invest in a marketing consultant at the outset, it's a wise move.

How do you go about finding the right outside advisers?

- Ask other business owners.
- Contact the professionals and ask for an appointment (a free consultation is often their best marketing ploy). Ask them for references and then follow up.
- Ask about their failures as well as their successes. Their responses will be revealing.
- How comfortable do you feel with them? The relationship with a professional doesn't have to be chummy, but you should feel confident in their discretion, integrity and concern for *your* business.
- If you already have a good relationship with your bank manager, ask him or her for recommendations. Many banks keep a referral list of professionals which they share with customers.
- Ask other professionals. For example, your family solicitor can refer you to a business lawyer.

Choose your business's legal structure

The legal structure of your business is an important choice, and it may be necessary to seek professional advice on the matter.

Many small businesses operate on a *sole trader* basis. The proprietor is the sole owner, personally liable for all debts, and pays tax on the profits. Businesses can start up at any time with no formalities. The accounting records do not have to comply with any legal requirements, nor need annual accounts be audited. It will, however, be essential to keep such records as are required by the Inland Revenue for Pay As You Earn purposes, and if your turnover exceeds the current threshold figure, to register for Value Added Tax with Customs and Excise. Expansion will be a problem if additional finance is required, and the business lapses with the owner's retirement, sickness or death.

Partnerships are more complex. The business is jointly owned by the partners, and *each* partner is personally liable for all the firm's debts, whether or not he or she was aware that they were being incurred. Otherwise, the tax and VAT requirements are as for a sole trader.

It is advisable to draw up a legal agreement before starting in business, otherwise any dispute or problem arising from incapacity, death, succession, difference of opinion, etc would be resolved in accordance with the Partnership Act of 1890, the terms of which might be contrary to your wishes.

Limited companies are a very convenient form of business. The company can survive the departure or death of directors by taking on new ones with minimal formalities so continuity is ensured, and finds it easier to raise finance than sole traders or partnerships. A limited company is well situated for future expansion, and can provide good benefits for its employers.

The accounts and annual returns must be prepared in accordance with the requirements of the Companies Acts, and filed annually. They are open to public inspection. The liability of the shareholders is limited to the share capital they have contributed, unless they have offered personal guarantees to the bank.

Disadvantages lie in the higher cost of National Insurance contributions and company taxation.

Set up bookkeeping, accounting, and office systems

The first step towards getting the operating information you will need to run your business is to make sure that you have the right kind of bookkeeping system.

Check with your trade association to see if they have any recommendations. While you will need your accountant's assistance to set up your bookkeeping and accounting systems, semi-customised systems may be available through your trade association. These will save you considerable time and money, as they make it unnecessary for you and your accountant to re-invent standard practices.

Choose your bookkeeping and accounting systems (with your accountant)

You have a wide range of choices in your bookkeeping and accounting systems. Some are low-cost, but demand a lot of your time. Most small business owners don't want to spend a lot of time being the bookkeeper and prefer to have someone in part time. Others prefer to use patented systems. Computerised systems are increasingly popular, and their cost is plummeting. Of course, PAYE, VAT and NI records must be kept in accordance with the requirements of governments.

Computerised systems are increasingly popular, and their cost is plummeting.

This is another choice that calls for professional advice. You want your system to provide accurate, timely information in a format that will help you manage your business better. You don't have to become a chartered accountant, but you should be familiar enough with standard financial accounting practices to be able to read and use a balance sheet, an income statement and a cash-flow budget. (See Chapter 5 for more on these.)

All bookkeeping systems require careful, accurate data entry. Your accountant or business adviser can help you to set up the books (decide what information to record and how to record it). But someone has to make those daily entries accurately as well as the summary accounting reports that convert the data into useful information.

You may find that a bookkeeping service is ideal. Shop around. Ask other similar businesses how they handle their bookkeeping and accounting and whether they are satisfied.

Accurate, timely information is so important in running a business that trying to economise in this area is like trying to economise on water when your house is on fire. Get the best assistance you can afford: it will be worth it. To paraphrase Peter Drucker, if you have to ask why you need an accountant, you aren't ready to go into business, and if you can't afford a good accountant, you don't have enough money to go into business.

Get business forms for interviewing, personnel records, etc

Keeping proper personnel records is almost as important as keeping proper tax and accounting records. At this time, set up your personnel records, including application and interview forms.

Keeping proper personnel records is almost as important as keeping proper tax and accounting records.

Ask your trade association. Get all the free leaflets available from the Department of Employment. If you can get application forms from large businesses (try simply asking), do so. They spend thousands of pounds to make sure they comply with the latest legal requirements. Best of all, take a course in basic personnel procedures.

Why is this so important?

- Employees have legal rights and you should be aware of them.
- Employers have legal responsibilities towards their staff.
- Some small business owners think 'I know how to deal with people' means having real personnel skills. This is not the case.
- Interviewing is a difficult skill to learn. It's easy to be swayed by our own preconceptions. Structured interviews are one way to minimise bias.

Record-keeping is another matter. You will need to keep records for tax and legal reasons, and it's far cheaper to do so correctly from the beginning than to reconstruct records at a later date. Ask your advisers, or a business lecturer who teaches personnel management, for help.

Determine your office equipment needs
How do you determine what office equipment you need? Ask people already in business. Don't rely on office supply salesmen to give you unbiased advice. The less you have to spend the better, but there will be some items you cannot do without. By making some of these decisions now, four months before opening, you can scout around for bargains and save some cash.

One of the great pleasures of owning a business is that it requires constant learning.

Take business courses

There are so many business courses that your problem may be where to start. In no special order, look into the following:

1. Financial management courses. These put bookkeeping and accounting information to work for you. You have to know how to read a balance sheet, a profit and loss account and cashflow projection. Ignoring financial management is a quick way to stunt your future.

2. Marketing courses. These include sales training, advertising

and other marketing skills. Marketing (the process of creating customers) is what business is all about. You can never learn too much about
how to attract and retain customers.

3. Personnel courses. Hiring, managing, assessing and even firing
personnel will probably be a constant challenge to you. Find out what
the basic practices are; there is no need to re-invent them.

4. Planning courses. Pre-business seminars are a good example.

One of the great pleasures of owning a business is that it requires
constant learning. Success comes from a host of incremental improvements: do this better, do that better . . . You don't have to master
everything. You do have to know enough to spot management
omissions.

Seek out and use demographic information

This is often called the Age of Information. What does that mean? First,
computers, surveys, census reports and studies abound. Second, he or
she who uses that information will prosper, while people who ignore it
or don't find time to use it won't. Third, information is inexpensive
power, and access to it is not that difficult.

**Information is
inexpensive power.**

Demographic information about your market includes such matters as
its age, gender, education and income level, location, buying habits and
hundreds of other factors. You use this information to identify
prospective customers, develop products and services to meet local needs
and make sound marketing choices. One easy use is to see how other
businesses segment their markets. Their insights might help you to steal
a march on your competitors.

The latest *Census of Population* (1981) gives the total population for each
town, classified by age, sex, social class, educational qualifications,
employment, unemployment, owner-occupiers, car owners and many
other details of value to business. Local volumes will possibly be in your
nearest main public library, or business library.

The *Guide to Official Statistics* indicates which government publications
are likely to be useful. They include the *Annual Abstract of Statistics*, which

shows increases and decreases in employment and production sectors. *Regional Trends* indicates the changes taking place in local employment, consumption, leisure and other areas of the economy.

Action Plan

Objective	Action/Strategy	Target date	Person responsible	Results/Comments
Select your business's name	Make list of possible names (asap)			
	Get list reviewed by outside advisers (within 30 days)			
	Choose name (30–45 days)			
Secure the best location for your business	Weigh costs, direct and indirect (30 days)			
	Review lease with solicitor before signing (asap)			
Establish business contacts	Join chamber of commerce (30–60 days)			
	Consider joining trade organisation (30–60 days)			
Expand your own information base	Continue to take business skills courses (ongoing)			
	Make appointments with outside advisers (within 10 days)			
	Select professional advisers (30 days)			
	Establish advisory board (within 60 days)			
Choose proper business structure	Consult solicitor, accountant (within 30 days)			
Establish good information flow	Consult accountant (asap)			
	Set up bookkeeping system			

Objective	Action/Strategy	Target date	Person responsible	Results/Comments
	Determine office equipment needs (30 days)			
Profit from demographic information	Visit public libraries or business libraries to consult government publications			
	Ask bankers, estate agents for local changes (occasional)			

CHAPTER 5

THREE MONTHS BEFORE START-UP

If you know what questions to ask, finding the answers is easy. Your financial statements will spell out a lot of answers about your business if you use professional advice in setting up your books, take steps to ensure that the information you receive is up to date and accurate, and use your financial statements to help you make decisions. Trying to take short cuts is folly. Unless you are a trained accountant (and even in this case I'd have serious reservations), invest as carefully in your information system as you do in employees and equipment. Your information system will help you to make the best use of these resources.

Invest as carefully in your information system as you do in employees and equipment.

Determine your cash needs

Strangely enough, financial analysis is the easiest part of your start-up planning. You have to put your business ideas into standardised formats, which have evolved over centuries to make information easy to analyse, compare and use. You may be unfamiliar with financial statements, but you are familiar with the kinds of question they can be used to answer. For example:

- How much cash do I need to start my business?
- Is this business going to be a good investment?
- Can I cover the wages every week?
- Will I make money?
- How much is my business worth?
- How does my business compare with other businesses?

- How many units must I sell to break even?
- Can I afford to buy this machine, hire that person, borrow more money, enter a new market?
- At what point will I be too deep in debt?

Your financial statements will help you to answer all these questions and more. You don't have to be a financial wizard to gain these benefits, since financial accounting is fairly straightforward. The more technical aspects can be handled by your accountant or other financial advisers, but the figures have to be based on *your* ideas.

This is particularly true during the start-up period, when the margin for error is very small. Once your business is up and running, your ideas will be corrected by experience. But now, the most you can hope for is to provide educated guesses based on your ideas, your research, and industry figures such as those provided by the various trade associations. These industry figures, which your bank manager or accountant can provide, will serve as your model.

At least make yourself familiar with the balance sheet (see Chapter 6) and the cash-flow projection. These will help you to answer the most pressing financial questions faced by start-ups. The profit and loss is useful too, but for start-up businesses the key question is: 'Do we have enough cash to meet our bills?' The answer to that comes from cash flow. The question 'Am I making a profit?' is secondary, because it doesn't matter whether or not you are making a profit if you can't pay your bills. Break-even analysis helps to quantify the sales levels you must reach based on your projected expenses and is used to decide how much a proposed addition (a new piece of equipment, a new employee, higher rent and so on) will really cost you. Ask your accountant or other financial advisers for help on break-even analysis, as it depends on some tricky judgements about expenses.

All these financial tools are important: financial control, using cash flow as a budget to hold down spending and the balance sheet to show the shifting balance between assets and liabilities, will spell the difference between making money and going broke.

Financial control will spell the difference between making money and going broke.

Review preliminary financial objectives

Even if you have altruistic motives for starting your business, you must still make a profit to remain in business in the long term. If you have come this far in your preparations for start-up, you must have good reasons to think your business will be profitable.

Set sales objectives

By this point, you've had plenty of time (and reasons) to alter your original sales objectives. One of the main reasons for getting as familiar as you can with your industry and questioning people experienced in your field is to avoid the dangers of setting unrealistic sales objectives. Later in this chapter, you will be able to forecast sales more precisely. For now, general answers to these questions are needed:

1. What range of sales do you think you will attain during the first year? This should be based on your research. An answer such as 'Between zero and £2,000,000' won't be much help. An answer such as '£50,000 to £250,000' will.

Cash sales = number of units × price. You may find it easier to think in terms of unit sales, chargeable hours per week or month, number of clients or other measures of sales than cash. For example, a hairdresser might think in terms of how many customers he or she might serve during an average week. A consultant might try to discover the average number of chargeable hours (as distinguished from the equally important non-chargeable time) per month. You get this kind of information by asking practitioners, experts in these fields and from trade publications. This is such a major problem that editors and writers can't leave it untouched.

2. What sales range do you want to hit in a few years? This can be very general, since it is used as a long-range target only.

Set profit objectives

The same thinking applies to profitability. Check industry figures, talk to owners of businesses like yours, and ask your bank manager and other financial advisers for an accurate picture. While they will be less optimistic than you, listen to them.

Many small business owners feel that pricing is the only way to compete.

Decide on your pricing strategies

Pricing is always frightening. Many small business owners feel that pricing is the only way to compete. You have a lot more choice in the matter of pricing now than you will have once you've implemented a pricing strategy, since how you set prices determines to some extent how the market perceives your company. The wrong perception can be harmful.

Price = Costs + Service + Image + Profit

Research pays off here. Your aim is to make sure your price structure is such that you make a profit, sell enough of your product or service to stay in business, and find a way to avoid price competition. In many ways, pricing is a balancing act. You have to balance image, perceived value, price sensitivity in your market and your own cost structures. The safest route is to establish a price range based on your business's costs, check the range against the competition, and keep a constant lookout for ways to sidestep price wars. You have many alternatives to price competition, not the least effective of which is staying out of price wars.

You have many alternatives to price competition, not the least effective of which is staying out of price wars.

Set sensible prices

Lack of courage in pricing is a common small business problem. Underpricing your goods or services (especially services) in order to gain market share is self-defeating. Low prices can actually deter prospects.

- Lower prices don't necessarily mean higher sales – but they do mean that you have to make more sales to reach the same cash totals. That may not be feasible.
- High quality and low prices don't fit well together; nor do low quality and high prices.
- If you don't think your service is valuable, why should your market?
- Raising prices is difficult, especially if you have established a reputation as a low-cost provider.
- Low-price strategies invite price competition in which everyone loses except the company with inordinately deep pockets.

Check what the market will bear

A good starting point for your pricing strategies is to look around.

- **What are other people charging?** Compare their prices with what you plan to charge. If your prices are going to be much higher or lower than average, be prepared to explain why you differ. Most experienced business owners are pretty careful about how they set prices and base much of their reasoning on experience.

- **At what point do higher prices drive customers away?** Try to find studies relevant to your business. Trade publications and advertising agencies can help.

- **Location affects prices.** The images of Bond Street, High Street and Discount Alley are very different.

Use price as a positioning tool

What image do you want to project? How do you want your goods or services to be perceived by your target markets? Price is a complex positioning tool, but it's one you have to use whether you want to or not.

Avoid competing on price alone

A good pricing strategy starts with costs and service level, then adds on elements of image (or positioning), and includes a profit component.

Some alternatives to price competition are:

- quality
- service
- value
- convenience
- delivery
- safety
- guarantees and warranties
- attractive financing options
- cleanliness

Don't make the mistake of underpricing in order to get customers.

Don't make the mistake of underpricing in order to get customers. It doesn't work.

Forecasting sales

Projecting sales is more art than science.

This is usually seen as the single most difficult part of financial projections. In many ways it is. Projecting sales is more art than science, and at best will be an imprecise affair. Too many outside factors affect sales levels: economic conditions, competition, changes in consumer and business buying patterns – even the weather. But you still have to estimate the level of sales your business will strive to reach.

Express your sales forecasts in pounds, bearing in mind that units sold times price equals total sales. You will use the sales forecast in both the projected profit and loss statement (P&L) and in your cash flow projection.

Use a three-column approach

The most effective and easiest way to project sales is to use a worst case/ best case/most likely case scenario. For a start-up business, this is even more difficult than for a going concern, since you don't have historical figures to guide your projections.

Break your goods and services down into small chunks. For example, you might use five product lines to cover the 150 products your store offers, or differentiate between professional and personal revenue sections of your consulting business rather than listing each client separately. A form similar to the one illustrated is useful. After estimating the gross sales figures in the worst case and best case scenarios, choose an in-between figure for the most likely. Add up the total of the 'most likely' column and spread it over the 12 months of the cash flow projection worksheet beginning on page 64.

	Worst case	Most likely case	Best case
A.	_____		
B.	_____		
C.	_____		
D.	_____		
E.	_____		
TOTAL:	_____	TOTAL: _____	TOTAL: _____

Figure 5.1 *Sales projection*

It is important to remember that these figures are at best educated guesses. As your business progresses, your guesses will become more educated and more accurate. If you err, try to err on the conservative side. If you estimate sales lower than they turn out to be, you'll be far

If you estimate sales lower than they turn out to be, you'll be far better off than if you pitch your estimate too high.

59

better off than if you pitch your estimate too high. Why? Because many expenses are geared to the sales forecast, and it is always easier to spend more than to save or cut back.

Seek assistance

Your accountant and other financial advisers will have had experience with businesses like yours and should be called on to help you make reasonable guesstimates. Ask for trade figures.

Trade association publications (ask the editor) sometimes run articles on how to forecast sales. If you can locate one of these, use it. What has worked for other people will work for you. Once you've been in business for a spell, you can safely try your own methods, but not now.

Many Small Firms Service and TEC advisers have had forecasting experience. So have some bank managers and consultants. Ask them. If they haven't done much forecasting, they won't be much help: good forecasting takes experience.

Decide your company's employee needs

Before trying to work out a P&L projection, look carefully at your sales forecast. It will help you to work out how many employees (if any) you should have when you start up. Since personnel is one of the largest expenses at this time, you don't want to add anyone to your staff without a strong business reason.

Some industries have a clear relation between employees and sales. A manufacturer might aim for £50,000 in sales per employee, while a distributor might look at five times that figure.

Look back at your visions of your business. How many employees are there? What are they doing? How much should they be paid? You can get local averages from the Department of Employment or a Jobcentre. Some industries have minimum rates laid down by Wages Councils for employees over 21, including boot and shoe repairing, hairdressing, laundry, retail food and allied trades.

Three questions that you should consider carefully are:

- How many employees do you need?
- When should you take them on?
- Can you afford to hire full-time employees? Can you use part-time help instead?

Put together an outside advisory board

Although most small business owners don't have a board of directors, most could benefit from an advisory board's objective oversight and advice. Successful business owners go to great lengths to get such boards together, and then heed the advice given.

Where would you find advisers? Ask those individuals you think could help you: they'll be flattered. The worst thing that could happen is that they'll say no. Talk to several of the following:

- Business friends
- Former employers or supervisors
- Retired business people from your industry
- Professionals
- Business lecturers
- Investors
- Consultants
- Experts in your field

Even one outside adviser will be invaluable. You will benefit from his or her experience and contacts; he or she benefits from involvement with a growing business. Even a personal friend who will listen to you intelligently makes a good sounding board. Business success comes from common sense and diligence. Outside advisers will help you to preserve both.

Project your cash flow

The cash flow projection, which you will use as a cash flow budget, makes you face business realities. Your cash flow budget will help you to hold down expenses and spot problems quickly. A business run without a budget lacks the discipline to survive, let alone prosper.

The nearest analogy to the cash flow budget is your current bank

Most small business owners could benefit from an advisory board's objective oversight and advice.

account. You don't record deposits until you put cash in (corresponding to cash inward). When you write a cheque you no longer have that money available (cash outward, or cash disbursement). You record disbursements when the cheque is actually written, not before. All cash transactions, including cheques, are recorded.

The key concepts concerning cash flow are amount and timing. Disbursements and inflows are time-dependent. You have to exercise some discretion over when you incur expenses. Probably the most common error people make during the start-up period is to anticipate cash revenues sooner than they should. The general rule is: cash will come in more slowly, and go out more rapidly, than you expect.

Here's how to create your own cash flow projection. Fill in the form on pages 64–65. If some of the lines don't apply to your business, or if you don't yet have the facts to hand, leave them blank. You can fill them in later. You want to make sure that cash inflows and outflows are shown in the months in which they fall. Remember: the keys to cash flow are amounts and timing.

Step 1. Start with the easy part. Fixed monthly payments can be reckoned accurately. These include rent, salaries and benefits, equipment rental payments, and any monthly term-loan payment.

Step 2. Payments that aren't necessarily made monthly, but whose size and timing can be scheduled, come next. Examples are ongoing advertising and marketing disbursements, some loan payments and equipment purchases.

Step 3. Predictable payments are largely discretionary, though some are necessary but sporadic (licences, for example). You have considerable choice over when to make most of these payments and will use these opportunities to juggle your cash flow.

Step 4. Now turn to the Cash Inflow section (lines 3 to 12). A separate section on projecting sales is given on page 59. Using the 'most likely' sales forecasts from there, try to spread out cash from sales and cash from receivables over the year. Each month will probably be different, depending on the seasonality of your business. Lines 7, 8, 9 and 10 (Debt,

Investment, Sale of fixed assets and Other) will be treated in Steps 8 and 9.

Seasonal patterns have such a dramatic effect on the shape of small business cash flow that you should seek expert advice on the pattern your business is most likely to face. Small business counsellors may be able to provide this advice free. You may also want to check local business college small business courses.

Seasonal patterns have a dramatic effect on the shape of small business cash flows.

Step 5. Variable payments depend on the level of sales. If sales are strong, you must have stock on hand to meet demand and may need extra help. Other variable costs will also increase. If sales are expected to be low, stocks can be low and other variable costs will shrink.

Step 6. Turn to Taxes, line 35. Ask your accountant for help. Taxes are part of the cost of doing business, and if you make money, you have to pay taxes. Their timing and amount vary – not at your whim but at the behest of the Inland Revenue.

Step 7. At this point, you can make the first cut at your cash flow. (It will change after you add back capital investment and proceeds from loans as outlined in the next two steps.) Work out the cash flow for each month: Net Cash Flow equals Total Cash Inflow minus Total Cash Outflow.

Step 8. Work out Cumulative Cash Flow for the entire first year. If it continues steadily downhill, keep projecting until the Cumulative Cash Flow definitely begins to turn up towards a positive figure. (If it never turns up, don't start the business unless your advisers can show you where your numbers have gone wrong.) For the first month, Cumulative Cash Flow equals Net Cash Flow (that is, line B41 equals B39). For the second month and beyond, add the new month's Net Cash Flow to the previous month's Cumulative Cash Flow to arrive at the new month's Cumulative Cash Flow.

You can now calculate how much capital your business needs (invested capital plus bank debt).

Cash Flow Projection Form

	A	B	C	D	E	F	G	H	I
		Jan	Feb	Mar	1 QTR	Apr	May	Jun	2 QTR
1		Jan	Feb	Mar	1 QTR	Apr	May	Jun	2 QTR
2									
3	Cash Inflow:								
4									
5	Cash sales								
6	Sales ledger								
7	Debt								
8	Investment								
9	Sale of fixed assets								
10	Other								
11									
12	Total Cash Inflow:								
13									
14	Cash Disbursements:								
15									
16	Owner salary								
17	Other salaries								
18	Licences								
19	Rent								
20	Utilities								
21	Phone								
22	Insurance								
23	Postage								
24	Advertising/Marketing								
25	Secretarial								
26	Travel								
27	Entertainment								
28	Equipment rental								
29	Office supplies								
30	Miscellaneous								
31	Start-up costs								
32	Term loan payments								
33									
34	Loan payments (other)								
35	Taxes								
36									
37	Total Cash Disbursements:								
38									
39	Net Cash Flow:								
40									
41	Cumulative Cash Flow:								
42									

Cash Flow Projection Form

	J	K	L	M	N	O	P	Q	R
1	Jul	Aug	Sep	3 QTR	Oct	Nov	Dec	4 QTR	Total: Year 1
2									
3									
4									
5									
6									
7									
8									
9									
10									
11									
12									
13									
14									
15									
16									
17									
18									
19									
20									
21									
22									
23									
24									
25									
26									
27									
28									
29									
30									
31									
32									
33									
34									
35									
36									
37									
38									
39									
40									
41									
42									

In all start-ups there are negative cash flows from the beginning because receipts take a while to come through.

In Step 4, certain cash inflows were deliberately left to be treated later. The reason is that in all start-ups there are negative cash flows from the beginning because receipts take a while to come through, while expenses start immediately. Inflows from new capital and loans cover these negative cash flows.

The Cumulative Cash Flow developed so far will typically show a pattern somewhat like this:

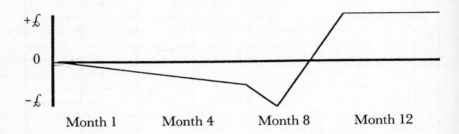

What causes this kind of pattern? Most start-ups start out slowly, with some initial business coming in from being the newcomer to the area. After a month or two, these sales dry up, and before sales start to increase again, significant sales and marketing efforts have to be made. These are expensive (see Month 8) and usually lead sales by a month or more.

Assess financial and capital needs

Step 9. Look for the lowest Cumulative Cash Flow in your projection. Multiply that figure by 150 per cent (1.5) to arrive at the capital your business will need. Why multiply it? To be safe. Money won't come in as fast as you hope, and you can bet on it going out faster than you feel comfortable with. The timing and amount of Cash Inflows needed from New Capital and Proceeds of Loans can now be calculated. The amount of cash from capital and loan proceeds should be spread out over the cash flow projection as needed. As a rule, capital comes in first. Then aim to borrow only as you must.

Meet your bank manager for preliminary talks whether or not you will use bank credit

Your bank manager will help to calculate your borrowing needs if you ask. Bring your cash flow statement and you will also establish your credibility in his or her eyes.

To minimise your costs, minimise borrowing. Use your cash flow projection to show your bank how much money you need, when, how you will pay it back, and why it is a good investment of the bank's money.

Step 10. Use the cash flow budget.
It is appallingly easy to spend too much on equipment, stock, interest or new personnel. A budget, consulted before any purchase, helps to keep spending down. You can always override it for compelling business reasons, but even then you would be wise to think twice.

A budget, consulted before any purchase, helps to keep spending down.

The simplest way to use the budget is to set up a form at the beginning of the month that has your projected figures in one column and actual figures in the other. At the end of the month, compare the two columns. If disbursements are down, find out why. It's easy to miss a payment or reduce stock without reordering. If disbursements are up, find out why. You may have prepaid a bill or overstocked. Then check inflows the same way. Look for variations; then seek the cause.

A case study

To help you understand the importance and usefulness of financial statements, consider the example of Hannah Kingman, who recently opened her own manufacturer's rep business in a medium-sized city. The following notes reflect her research into the business and her two years of experience working for another manufacturer's rep in an allied though not directly competitive field.

Some important points are:

● *Hannah's start-up was planned over a period of several years.* Her initial steps involved researching businesses that appealed to her. Distribution businesses, manufacturer's reps, service businesses, and consulting had the closest fit with her interests, experience and goals. She decided to become a manufacturer's rep because it offers rewards tied directly to her efforts and abilities, allows her to manage her own time, has low capital needs, and because she talked to some reps who heartily enjoyed their work.

● *Hannah took time to gain experience before leaping into business for herself.* That experience is difficult to overvalue. She learned how to work with principals (the manufacturers whose product lines she represents), how to identify prospects and decide which ones to approach, what the pitfalls of a rep business are, and (most important of all) how to make money in a notoriously competitive business. She also was paid for her efforts and was able to tuck away enough cash to make sure that when she did begin her business, she'd be able to survive until the business could support her.

● *She will use her own money to get started.* Initially she plans to work out of her house and car to keep her overhead low. A mortgage is one way to spring money out of a house. Windfalls (inheritances, winning at the racetrack, a bonus or profit share, and so forth) could also be used, but most successful small business owners don't rely on luck. They plan for their success. So does Hannah.

● *Hannah availed herself of all the help she could get.* Although her degree in English didn't teach her how to read financial statements and run a business, it did teach her research skills. She took a pre-business course and wrote a comprehensive business plan. She took a few sales courses, and since she wants to expand her business, she continues to take management courses and read trade publications.

● *Hannah set goals and made sure she achieved them.* Directed efforts are more productive than yearning. She knew that if she were to be her own boss she had some hurdles to leap: gaining skill and experience, acquiring capital, meeting people and forming business relationships. You don't just walk into a manufacturer and say, 'Good morning, I'd like to represent your product lines. . . .'

● *Hannah's financial model starts with a sales forecast and worksheet.* This approach is more detailed than for many start-ups, but because she gained access to more information she felt she could predict her start-up sales patterns and running expenses with considerable accuracy. She also uses a profit and loss projection (P&L) as an intermediate step in establishing her cash flow budget. You won't necessarily have to do this for your start-up, but it is recommended.

● **_Hannah forecasts sales and expenses for three years._** She plans to add staff in the second year, which will dramatically change her business.

Hannah's sales forecast

Hannah represents several storage unit, display case, and shelving manufacturers. She learned that there were three markets: institutional (schools, hospitals, etc), retail stores and industrial firms. Sales split 20/80 between office and display uses, with over 40 per cent of the sales coming from the retail sector. The remaining sales should split evenly between institutional and industrial markets. This detailed information can only come from careful research. A combination of trade association and individual sales reps' experience provided the basis for her conclusions.

Based on her experience in a closely related business (as well as trade information), she can predict what her sales pattern will be after she is established. Her business has seasonal fluctuations that can be anticipated and planned for.

The three forecasts are based on attaining market share the first year. The anticipated total sales in her industry, for her market area, will be £3.5 million. She thinks she can get a minimum of 10 per cent and a maximum of 20 per cent of the market the first year. She can then calculate total sales, which represents the sum of all sales she brings in for the companies she represents. Spread among market segments, and with high and low ranges established, she chose a more probable 14 per cent figure ('Most likely') as a base for her plans.

Trade commission rates in her field average 15 per cent. The revenue for Hannah's business is calculated by multiplying total sales by 15 per cent.

Expenses are calculated on the Sales Forecast Worksheet to total £57,000 the first year. The profit or loss is simply receipts minus expenses.

Hannah's Sales Forecast Worksheet

Sales forecasting	Worst case 10% mkt share £	Most likely 14% mkt share £	Best case 20% mkt share £
Office			
Institutional	20,000	28,000	40,000
Retail	30,000	42,000	60,000
Industrial	20,000	28,000	40,000
Display			
Institutional	80,000	112,000	160,000
Retail	120,000	168,000	240,000
Industrial	80,000	112,000	160,000
Total:	350,000	490,000	700,000
Revenues (15% commission rate):	52,500	73,500	105,000
Expenses (from worksheet):	57,000	57,000	57,000
Profit (Loss):	(4,500)	16,500	48,000

Sales pattern (based on experience and trade information):

1st quarter	15%	£11,025
2nd quarter	30%	£22,050
3rd quarter	20%	£14,700
4th quarter	35%	£25,725

Hannah's Expense Forecast

This worksheet gives an overview of Hannah's expenses and determines the sales level needed to meet those expenses (break-even point). The line items aren't exhaustive, but cover all the major expenses Hannah will be facing.

Salary. Hannah wants to make £24,000 her first year, £30,000 the second, £36,000 the third.

Licences, life and medical insurance etc. Estimated as 40 per cent of salary total. In Years 2 and 3, this includes salaries and benefits for new employees.

Her other expense figures are estimates, based on trade figures, experience, and conversations with other sales reps in similar lines.

Total monthly. Sum of lines 8 to 22.

Total full year. Line 24 times 12.

Break-even. Line 26 divided by 15 per cent (the commission rate). In order to cover expenses, sales have to be £392,000 or better for the year. Since her sales forecast showed £490,000 as the most likely first year sales figure, Hannah has a comfortable margin. This is a very handy feasibility analysis. It shows that Hannah's business goals are within reach and gives a clear go-ahead sign.

Years 2 and 3: If Hannah adds another salesperson and a secretary to free her own time for more aggressive sales in the second year, she expects to achieve results as shown. Sales would have to more than double for her to break even. Is this realistic? Hannah believes it is, but plans to wait until she has more experience running her own business before committing to this growth.

		Year 1	Year 2	Year 3
1.				
2.	Costs	£4,900.00	£12,128.17	£13,386.86
3.	Monthly gross sales	32,666.67	80,854.44	89,245.71
4.	Gross sales	392,000.00	970,253.33	1,070,948.53
5.				
6.				
7.	EXPENSES (Monthly)			
8.	Salary (owner)	£2,000.00	£2,500.00	£3,000.00
9.	Salaries (other)	0.00	3,803.33	4,031.53
10.	Licences, insurances etc.	800.00	2,521.33	2,812.61
11.	Rent	250.00	265.00	280.90
12.	Utilities	75.00	79.50	84.27
13.	Insurance	150.00	159.00	168.54
14.	Phone	250.00	397.50	421.35
15.	Mail etc	100.00	159.00	168.54
16.	Adv/Mktg	150.00	318.00	337.08
17.	Secretarial	200.00	212.00	224.72
18.	Travel	600.00	1,272.00	1,348.32
19.	Entertainment	50.00	150.00	200.00
20.	Equipment rental	125.00	132.50	140.45
21.	Office supplies	50.00	53.00	56.18
22.	Miscellaneous	100.00	106.00	112.36
23.				
24.	Total monthly	£4,900.00	£12,128.17	£13,386.86
25.				
26.	Total full year	£58,800.00	£145,538.00	£160,642.28
27.				
28.	Break-even	£392,000.00	£970,253.33	£1,070,948.53

Hannah's Profit and Loss Projection

	A	B	C	D	E	F
1		Jan	Feb	Mar	Apr	May
2	Income:					
3	Office	500	1,000	1,200	1,600	1,800
4	Display	1,200	2,000	3,000	3,600	6,000
5	Total Income:	1,700	3,000	4,200	5,200	7,800
6						
7	Quarters:			8,900		
8						
9	Expenses:					
10	Owner salary	2,000	2,000	2,000	2,000	2,000
11	Salaries (other)	0	0	0	0	0
12	Licences	800	800	800	800	800
13	Insurance	150	150	150	150	150
14	Rent	250	250	250	250	250
15	Utilities	75	75	75	75	75
16	Phone	250	250	250	250	250
17	Mail	100	100	100	100	100
18	Advertising/Marketing	150	150	150	150	150
19	Secretarial	200	200	200	200	200
20	Travel	600	600	600	600	600
21	Entertainment	50	50	50	50	50
22	Equipment lease	125	125	125	125	125
23	Office supplies	50	50	50	50	50
24	Miscellaneous	100	100	100	100	100
25						
26	Interest					
27						
28	Total Expenses:	4,900	4,900	4,900	4,900	4,900
29						
30	Profit (Loss):	(3,200)	(1,900)	(700)	300	2,900
31						
32						
33	Sales Pattern (based on experience and trade information):					
34		1 Qtr	15%		11,025	
35		2 Qtr	30%		22,050	
36		3 Qtr	20%		14,700	
37		4 Qtr	35%		25,725	

Hannah's Profit and Loss Projection

	G	**H**	**I**	**J**	**K**	**L**	**M**	**N**
1	Jun	Jul	Aug	Sep	Oct	Nov	Dec	TOTAL
2								
3	2,000	1,700	500	700	1,200	1,800	3,000	17,000
4	7,000	5,400	2,400	4,000	6,500	7,500	7,000	55,600
5	9,000	7,100	2,900	4,700	7,700	9,300	10,000	73,500
6								
7	22,000			14,700			27,000	
8								
9								
10	2,000	2,000	2,000	2,000	2,000	2,000	2,000	24,000
11	0	0	0	0	0	0	0	0
12	800	800	800	800	800	800	800	9,600
13	150	150	150	150	150	150	150	1,800
14	250	250	250	250	250	250	250	3,000
75	75	75	75	75	75	75	75	900
16	250	250	250	250	250	250	250	3,000
17	100	100	100	100	100	100	100	1,200
18	150	150	150	150	150	150	150	1,800
19	200	200	200	200	200	200	200	2,400
20	600	600	600	600	600	600	600	7,200
21	50	50	50	50	50	50	50	600
22	125	125	125	125	125	125	125	1,500
23	50	50	50	50	50	50	50	600
24	100	100	100	100	100	100	100	1,200
25								
26								
27								
28	4,900	4,900	4,900	4,900	4,900	4,900	4,900	58,800
29								
30	4,100	2,200	(2,000)	(200)	2,800	4,400	5,100	13,800
31								
32								
33								
34								
35								
36								
37								

Hannah's projected profit and loss

A P&L projection is based on anticipated revenues and expenses as they are incurred, unlike their treatment in a cash flow projection, where they are booked only when cash is exchanged. A P&L is used to determine whether or not your small business is making money and is optional until you are actually in business. The real key to survival is cash flow: you can go broke while making money if the cash isn't coming in as fast as it goes out.

Hannah's P&L projection is for one year and is used to support her cash flow projection. Some of the major differences between the cash flow and the income statement revolve around non-cash expenses (depreciation, amortisation) that are reported on a P&L but not on the cash flow, while some cash disbursements (loan repayments including principal and interest) appear on the cash flow but not on the P&L.

Line 5: Total Income. Anticipated revenues of £73,500 (from the sales forecast) are spread over 12 months according to the anticipated pattern.

Lines 10 to 24: Expenses. Anticipated expenses of £58,800 (from the worksheet) are distributed evenly over the 12 months.

Line 30: Profit (Loss) is shown monthly. A monthly P&L can be misleading, especially in a start-up business. Quarterly P&Ls are actually more useful, as they allow the surges and anomalies to even out. Studying three months at a time (current month plus the two immediately previous months) is even more handy. Profit is simply Total Income minus Total Expenses (line 5 minus line 28). Projected first year profit: £13,800.

Lines 34 to 37: Note the sales pattern provided at the bottom of the P&L. This is the same pattern as shown on the sales forecast.

Hannah's Asset List and Values

Hannah's asset list includes display stock (she has to maintain a sales room), necessary office equipment (some of which she owns, some of which will be purchased during the first year and show up on the cash flow), and a parcel of licences that are part of the cost of doing business.

This information will be used to support the cash flow projection and balance sheet.

Asset List and Values	£	£
Display stock		
Opening stock	2,000	
New stock	5,000	
Total stock		7,000
Office equipment:		
copier	700	
computer & software	3,700	
printer	2,000	
typewriter	400	
filing cabinets	600	
telephones	1,200	
car phone (cellular)	600	
answering machine	300	
Total Office Equipment		9,500
Licences, insurance		1,000
TOTAL		17,500

Hannah's Cash Flow Projections

Two projections are presented on pages 78–81: an initial cash flow (to show where the holes are) and a revised cash flow (which reflects needed capital investment and new debt). This two-step approach is highly recommended, as it allows you to calculate with some accuracy how much you need to invest and/or borrow and when that cash will be needed in the business.

A cash flow projection is based on amounts of cash and the timing of that cash's movement. Balancing cash flow is a major survival skill for a small business, especially if access to additional capital or debt is in question.

Line 5: Cash sales are sales paid for at the time. Unlike the P&L, where sales are booked when made regardless of the payment schedule, cash flow projections demand that money (including cheques) changes hands.

Line 6: Sales ledger has been calculated according to a rather complex schedule. Hannah's schedule is based on two patterns: office sales are 50 per cent cash, 50 per cent in 30 days; display sales are 50 per cent cash, 50 per cent in 90 days. Your pattern will depend on your business. In Hannah's example, her research and experience suggested that she take a conservative approach. (She really expects the sales ledger to be significantly shorter, which would accelerate her cash flow.)

Line 7: Debt. No debt is shown on the preliminary cash flow, because Hannah didn't know how much to borrow or when. That decision is made by looking at lines 39 and 41, Cash Flow and Cumulative Cash Flow.

Line 8: Investment. Similar considerations apply to new investment. Hannah's combination of debt and investment is based on her analysis of the preliminary cash flow projection, equipment needs, and disbursement patterns. She had her banker and accountant help her make these decisions.

Line 16: Salary. Hannah plans to take £1,000 a month at first, then increase it as the business takes off.

Line 18: Taxes and benefits. Currently figured at 40 per cent of salary, these will increase as her salary goes up.

Line 19: Rent payments don't start until the third month.

Line 20: Utilities are a space cost, so they too are postponed.

Line 21: Phone costs are based on anticipated use: heavy at first, then following a well-known pattern.

Line 22: Insurance is paid quarterly. Compare with the P&L, as insurance is used evenly throughout the year. This kind of difference between the P&L and cash flow is important to understand.

Line 23: Postage. Heavy, then light. Start-up mailing is expensive.

Line 24: Advertising/Marketing. An initial blitz, including direct mail, will get Hannah's firm off the ground. After that, advertising and marketing costs are governed by two factors: ongoing marketing expenses and special promotions.

Line 25: Secretarial. Part-time help, as needed.

Line 26: Travel. Seasonal adjustments.

Line 27: Entertainment. Ditto.

Line 28: Equipment Rental. Monthly payments.

Line 30: Miscellaneous. January includes £200 of small items as well as equipment to the tune of £9,500 (see asset list). In April, £5,000 of new inventory will be needed.

Line 31: Start-up Costs. In January, licences and fees plus starting inventory.

Line 32: Term Loan Payments.

Line 34: Loan Payments (other). A May payment of £5,000 will cover some pre-start-up costs Hannah incurred, including her own car.

Line 35: Taxes. None anticipated the first year.

Line 37: Total Cash Disbursements. Total of lines 16 to 35.

Line 39: Cash Flow. Line 12 (Total Cash Inflow) minus line 37. Monthly figures used to check progress.

Line 41: Cumulative Cash Flow. Used as a guide to when new debt or capital is needed, when debt can be repaid, and similar major financial decisions.

Notes on Hannah's Cash Flow Projection

In Hannah's preliminary cash flow, negative cash flow peaks in the second quarter at -£25,425. Hannah uses this information to make some important decisions:

Hannah's Preliminary Cash Flow Projection

	A	B	C	D	E	F	G	H	I
1		Jan	Feb	Mar	1 QTR	Apr	May	Jun	2 QTR
2		(15,125)	(16,100)	(16,525)	(16,525)	(21,825)	(25,425)	(21,500)	(21,500)
3	Cash Inflow:								
4									
5	Cash sales	850	1,500	2,100	4,450	2,600	3,900	4,500	11,000
6	Sales ledger		850	1,500	2,350	2,100	2,600	3,900	8,600
7	Debt				0				0
8	Investment				0				0
9	Sale of fixed assets				0				0
10	Other				0				0
11									
12	Total Cash Inflow:	850	2,350	3,600	6,800	4,700	6,500	8,400	19,600
13									
14	Cash Disbursements:								
15									
16	Owner salary	1,000	1,000	1,500	3,500	2,000	2,000	2,000	6,000
17	Other salaries	0	0	0	0	0	0	0	0
18	Licences	400	400	600	1,400	800	800	800	2,400
19	Rent	0	0	250	250	250	250	250	750
20	Utilities	0	0	125	125	100	75	50	225
21	Phone	350	200	300	850	350	300	250	900
22	Insurance	0	800	0	800	0	0	0	0
23	Postage	200	100	100	400	125	100	100	325
24	Advertising/Marketing	600	0	50	650	150	150	100	400
25	Secretarial	100	150	200	450	200	200	200	600
26	Travel	300	400	600	1,300	750	750	600	2,100
27	Entertainment	50	100	100	250	100	100	0	200
28	Equipment rental	125	125	125	375	125	125	125	375
29	Office supplies	150	0	25	175	50	50	0	100
30	Miscellaneous	9,700	50	50	9,800	5,000	200	0	5,200
31	Start-up costs	3,000							
32	Term loan payments				0				0
33									
34	Loan payments (other)				0		5,000		5,000
35	Taxes				0				0
36									
37	Total Cash Disbursements:	15,975	3,325	4,025	23,325	10,000	10,100	4,475	24,575
38									
39	Cash Flow:	(15,125)	(975)	(425)	(16,525)	(5,300)	(3,600)	3,925	(4,975)
40									
41	Cumulative Cash Flow:	(15,125)	(16,100)	(16,525)	(16,525)	(21,825)	(25,425)	(21,500)	(21,500)
42									

Hannah's Preliminary Cash Flow Projection

	J	K	L	M	N	O	P	Q	R
1	Jul	Aug	Sep	3 QTR	Oct	Nov	Dec	4 QTR	Total: Year 1
2	(17,575)	(17,950)	(18,675)	(18,675)	(17,250)	(14,325)	(9,775)	(9,775)	
3									
4									
5	3,550	1,450	2,350	7,350	3,850	4,650	5,000	13,500	36,300
6	4,500	3,550	1,450	9,500	2,350	3,850	4,650	10,850	31,300
7				0				0	0
8				0				0	0
9				0				0	0
10				0				0	0
11									
12	8,050	5,000	3,800	16,850	6,200	8,500	9,650	24,350	67,600
13									
14									
15									
16	2,000	2,000	2,000	6,000	2,000	2,000	2,000	6,000	21,500
17	0	0	0	0	0	0	0	0	0
18	800	800	800	2,400	800	800	800	2,400	8,600
19	250	250	250	750	250	250	250	750	2,500
20	50	50	50	150	100	175	125	400	900
21	150	150	200	500	250	300	250	800	3,050
22	0	800	0	800	300	0	0	300	1,900
23	50	50	150	250	100	75	50	225	1,200
24	50	350	100	500	0	300	150	450	2,000
25	100	200	200	500	200	350	300	850	2,400
26	450	500	500	1,450	500	750	800	2,050	6,900
27	50	50	100	200	50	100	100	250	900
28	125	125	125	375	125	125	125	375	1,500
29	0	50	0	50	0	250	50	300	625
30	50	0	50	100	100	100	100	300	15,400
31									
32				0				0	0
33									
34				0				0	5,000
35				0				0	0
36									
37	4,125	5,375	4,525	14,025	4,775	5,575	5,100	15,450	77,375
38									
39	3,925	(375)	(725)	2,825	1,425	2,925	4,550	8,900	(9,775)
40									
41	(17,575)	(17,950)	(18,675)	(18,675)	(17,250)	(14,325)	(9,775)	(9,775)	
42									

Hannah's Revised Cash Flow Projection

	A	B	C	D	E	F	G	H	I
1		Jan	Feb	Mar	1 QTR	Apr	May	Jun	2 QTR
2		(125)	(1,100)	(1,525)	(1,525)	5,675	2,075	11,000	11,000
3	Cash Inflow:								
4									
5	Cash sales	850	1,500	2,100	4,450	2,600	3,900	4,500	11,000
6	Sales ledger		850	1,500	2,350	2,100	2,600	3,900	8,600
7	Debt				0	12,500		5,000	17,500
8	Investment	15,000			15,000				0
9	Sale of fixed assets				0				0
10	Other				0				0
11									
12	Total Cash Inflow:	15,850	2,350	3,600	21,800	17,200	6,500	13,400	37,100
13									
14	Cash Disbursements:								
15									
16	Owner salary	1,000	1,000	1,500	3,500	2,000	2,000	2,000	6,000
17	Other salaries	0	0	0	0	0	0	0	0
18	Licences	400	400	600	1,400	800	800	800	2,400
19	Rent	0	0	250	250	250	250	250	750
20	Utilities	0	0	125	125	100	75	50	225
21	Phone	350	200	300	850	350	300	250	900
22	Insurance	0	0	0	800	0	0	0	800
23	Postage	200	100	100	400	125	100	100	325
24	Advertising/Marketing	600	0	50	650	150	150	100	400
25	Secretarial	100	150	200	450	200	200	200	600
26	Travel	300	400	600	1,300	750	750	600	2,100
27	Entertainment	50	100	100	250	100	100	0	200
28	Equipment rental	125	125	125	375	125	125	125	375
29	Office supplies	150	0	25	175	50	50	0	100
30	Miscellaneous	9,700	50	50	9,800	5,000	200	0	5,200
31	Start-up costs	3,000							
32	Term loan payments				0				0
33									
34	Loan payments (other)				0		5,000		5,000
35	Taxes				0				0
36									
37	Total Cash Disbursements:	15,975	3,325	4,025	23,325	10,000	10,100	4,475	24,575
38									
39	Cash Flow:	(125)	(975)	(425)	(1,525)	7,200	(3,600)	8,925	12,525
40									
41	Cumulative Cash Flow:	(125)	(1,100)	(1,525)	(1,525)	5,675	2,075	11,000	11,000

Hannah's Revised Cash Flow Projection

	J	K	L	M	N	O	P	Q	R
1	Jul	Aug	Sep	3 QTR	Oct	Nov	Dec	4 QTR	Total: Year 1
2	8,355	7,910	7,115	7,115	6,970	4,825	9,375	9,375	
3									
4									
5	3,550	1,450	2,350	7,350	3,850	4,650	5,000	13,500	36,300
6	4,500	3,550	1,450	9,500	2,350	3,850	4,650	10,850	31,300
7				0				0	17,500
8				0				0	15,000
9				0				0	0
10				0				0	0
11									
12	8,050	5,000	3,800	16,850	6,200	8,500	9,650	24,350	100,100
13									
14									
15									
16	2,000	2,000	2,000	6,000	2,000	2,000	2,000	6,000	21,500
17	0	0	0	0	0	0	0	0	0
18	800	800	800	2,400	800	800	800	2,400	8,600
19	250	250	250	750	250	250	250	750	2,500
20	50	50	50	150	100	175	125	400	900
21	150	150	200	500	250	300	250	800	3,050
22	0	0	0	800	0	0	0	300	1,900
23	50	50	150	250	100	75	50	225	1,200
24	50	350	100	500	0	300	150	450	2,000
25	100	200	200	500	200	350	300	850	2,400
26	450	500	500	1,450	500	750	800	2,050	6,900
27	50	50	100	200	50	100	100	250	900
28	125	125	125	375	125	125	125	375	1,500
29	0	50	0	50	0	250	50	300	625
30	50	0	50	100	100	100	100	300	15,400
31									
32	70	70	70	210	70	70	0	140	350
33									
34	6,500			6,500	1,500	5,000		6,500	18,000
35				0				0	0
36									
37	10,695	5,445	4,595	20,735	6,345	10,645	5,100	22,090	90,725
38									
39	(2,645)	(445)	(795)	(3,885)	(145)	(2,145)	4,550	2,260	9,375
40									
41	8,355	7,910	7,115	7,115	6,970	4,825	9,375	9,375	

● She will need to invest £15,000 in January to get her business off to a safe start.

● Even with this investment, things will be tight in the second quarter so she plans to borrow £12,500 after consulting her bank manager and accountant. If she doesn't have to borrow this amount, she won't, but by planning for it before start-up, she knows it will be available to her if she needs it and if the rest of her assumptions work out. If they don't, she stands to lose some or all of her investment and doesn't want to compound that problem.

● Cash flow should then improve dramatically, so Hannah plans to repay the loan: £6,500 in July, £1,500 in October, and £5,000 in November. This includes interest payments as well as principal.

These changes are reflected in the revised cash flow projection, which will also function as her cash flow budget.

Action Plan

Objective	Action/Strategy	Target date	Person responsible	Results/Comments
Establish rough financial objectives	Get industry figures (10 days)			
	Ask bank, accountant for parameters (10 days)			
Establish pricing strategies	Check current market (ongoing)			
	Work out your probable costs (asap)			
	Look for ways to increase perceived value (ongoing)			
	Check with trade sources (30 days)			
Establish a rational sales forecast	Research trade information (10 days)			
	Prepare three-column analysis (within 2 weeks)			
Establish personnel plan	Prepare list of jobs (10 to 20 days)			
	Research salary levels (10 days)			
	Check with small business advisers (within 30 days)			
Determine capital needs	Consult with accountant (asap)			
	Prepare cash flow forecast (within 2 weeks)			
	Review cash flow forecast with accountant, bank (20 to 30 days)			

◀ CHAPTER 6 ▶

TWO MONTHS BEFORE START-UP

Basic marketing plans include product/service benefits, target marketing and watchful concern for the competition. Reviewing the non-financial objectives and sales forecasts helps to ensure that your latest thinking governs your projections. Securing finance and insurance cover takes longer than many anticipate – two months is not too long a time to plan on. Financing will be dependent on your sales and cash flow assumptions, so they should be carefully annotated, even if no outside finance will be required. Your money is important too.

Prepare your marketing plan

A marketing plan helps you to work out ways to find and keep customers.

A marketing plan helps you to work out ways to find and keep customers, reach your sales goals and keep your business efforts concentrated on those areas which will be most lucrative (both in the short and long term). It is built around your customers: their product and service preferences, their perception of your business and their changing interests.

This should not be a major literary effort. Answer the questions, and keep asking and answering them as you go along.

Know your markets; know your products/services and the benefits they offer; and know your competition. This is information at work.

Continue to pursue a clearer definition, acquiring a more detailed knowledge of the people who compose your target markets. You can never know your markets too well.

Answer these minimum questions about your average prospect:

- How old?
- Male or female?
- What educational level?
- What income?
- What occupation?
- What buying preferences (in your kind of business)?
- What products, services and benefits do they (might they) buy from you?
- What buying patterns?
- How can you profitably reach them (through which promotion and advertising avenues)?
- If industrial sales, what title or department?
- And, most important: how can you find more people like them?

Answer these questions and keep asking them, and your competition will be left behind. For some reason, very few small business owners are willing to ask and answer these questions on an ongoing basis. It takes work, but work makes winners. You can get help from TEC, the Small Firms Service, your suppliers, and most of all from your own observation and research. If you find that you aren't keeping up with this research, question your motivation for going into business. Markets are not static: they change. The business owner who is prepared for these changes wins.

Markets change. The business owner who is prepared for these changes wins.

Make a product/service benefits list

You may think you sell a service or a product. Your customers buy benefits. For each product or service that you plan to sell, list the possible benefits that a purchaser would gain.

Features and benefits are closely related, but have to be kept separate. Features are used to describe what you sell: a service may be fast, cost-effective, available six days a week. A product may be made of wood and steel. Those are all features. Benefits, on the other hand, describe why the customer is buying your product or service. He or she wants convenience, economy and durability.

85

For each product or service you offer, how would your customer answer the question: 'What's in it for me?'

A benefits list helps you to keep advertising costs down (advertising agencies need to know what's in it for the customer), make product or service decisions (by concentrating on your market's desires, not your preferences), and beat the competition (they won't normally be keeping the customers' preferences in mind). The basic idea is to make sure that you offer only what your market wants to buy.

Your research (both hot and cool) should have given you a good idea of what your markets want. Some ideas come from research into competitors, some from questioning suppliers, some from trade research. The big danger is to assume that you represent your markets' tastes so well that this research is not needed. That's the best way to stock up on skateboards or frisbees or eight-track tape decks.

Is your research thorough and up to date?

For retailers
Set up supplier files. Vendors will help you to make better purchasing decisions. They have a vested interest in your success, they know (more or less) what other people are buying, and they can help you to learn how to spot items that will sell.

Supplier files are simple. Use a manila folder for each supplier's product and price-lists, advertising material and any other information you come across. Understand your suppliers (and their problems), and you will gain better terms.

What are the usual terms for new entrants to this business? Investigate order cycles: how long from order to shelf? Once you are established, you will find trade credit (buying on terms) a strong financing tool. At this point, you will probably have to pay cash, but check with suppliers anyway. Some will help you to get started – especially if you can show them how their investment in your business will pay off.

Set up competitor files

Your competition is just as clever and motivated as you are. Some of them are better established; some will be better financed, have more experience or have other advantages over you. What can you do to fight back?

Your competition is just as clever and motivated as you are.

Keep track of everything your nearest competitors do. Keep records of their ads, their promotions, their financial dealings. If they add a branch office or close a satellite operation or merge with another business, you need to know. Competitor files are simply manila folders, one for each competitor, which you use to store the information you gather.

Keep these files up to date and review them periodically, and you will know more about your competitors than they know about themselves. When do they have sales? What benefits do they stress? Are they going after new target markets, or trying to buy market share, or competing on quality? Are they consistent or scatterbrained? What are their staff like: polite? haughty? well trained? slovenly? Study them. Ring them and note how they answer the phone.

Know your competitors so well that you know what they will do before they do.

Review non-financial objectives: image

Your business image will be developed by (among other factors) your markets, quality of product lines or service, price strategy, location, personnel and advertising/promotion efforts.

Advertising/promotion includes stationery, business cards, signboards, and public relations as well as ads and brochures. Many new business owners skimp on these apparently secondary areas, but it's an expensive economy. You only get one chance to make a first impression, and once that impression has been made it's hard (and costly) to change your image.

- **Product/service and markets.** Test for a 'fit'. Certain market segments want certain products or services. Buyers of business services, for example, are more interested in experience, stability and demonstrated competence than in price. Quality or level of service is

Customers like consistency. Give it to them.

one important fit; price is another; convenience is yet another. The list is long – but if you know your markets, your products/services and what image you want to project, you should be able to come up with your own list of fitting criteria. You want to make sure you don't offer something that jars with your principal marketing efforts. Customers like consistency. Give it to them.

- **Location.** You chose your location with marketing uppermost in your mind. Improvements to the premises should continue along the same track. Will the premises (office or shop) be what your market expects and will appreciate? The decor should be chosen to please the customers, not you.

- **Employees.** Hiring the right employees in the first place is simpler than hiring the wrong employees, then trying to remould them.

  - What kind of employees does your market expect?
  - Whom does the competition hire?
  - What is normal? (Unless you have extremely strong reasons to deviate from the norm, don't.)
  - What educational level is required?
  - How should employees dress?
  - How important is grooming and appearance to the function of the job?
  - What training would help to differentiate your employees from everyone else's?
  - Should your employees be local, or doesn't it matter?

Your employees represent your business to the public. Once again, place your market's preferences and expectations ahead of your own. They're the ones who will pay the bills.

Review sales forecasts

As the start-up date approaches, go over your sales forecasts again. You may have gleaned some information that would cause you to change your original estimates, and when you sit down with your bank manager (or your backers, including family or friends), you want to make sure your forecasts are conservative. If you sales forecasts have changed, your cash flow forecast will change too. Your updated thinking has to be reflected in your cash flow projection.

Prepare a preliminary balance sheet

A well-prepared balance sheet is mandatory. Your banker needs it. You need it. Your accountant or bookkeeping service will need it. A balance sheet, like cash flow, is a tool to help you to manage your business better. The balance sheet is often compared to a snapshot bearing a date: it shows what your company looks like at a given moment.

The balance sheet is often compared to a snapshot: it shows what your company looks like at a given moment.

The balance sheet weighs what you own (assets) against what you owe (liabilities). The difference between assets and liabilities is the net worth (owner's equity), sometimes used in working out the value of the business.

The balance sheet

ASSETS	LIABILITIES
Current Assets	**Current Liabilities**
Cash	Taxes payable
Notes receivable	Salaries payable
Sales ledger	Notes/Loans payable
Stock for sale	Bought ledger
Other stock	Current portion long term
Debtors	***Total Current Liabilities***
Supplies	
Prepaid expenses	**Long-Term Liabilities**
Total Current Assets	Notes
	Term loans
Fixed Assets	Mortgage
Property	Loans from directors
Fixtures and leasehold	***Total Long-Term Liabilities***
improvements	
Equipment	***Total Liabilities***
Vehicles	
Goodwill	**Net Worth**
Other	Subordinated debt
Total Fixed Assets	Retained earnings
	Invested capital
TOTAL ASSETS:	
	TOTAL LIABILITIES
	AND NET WORTH:

The format of the balance sheet is governed by a simple rule: assets and liabilities are both listed in order of their immediacy. Those assets that are nearest to cash are listed ahead of those assets that are used to maintain the business (the so-called fixed assets). Those liabilities that are nearest to being due are listed ahead of long-term debt, and all liabilities are listed ahead of the permanent capital (invested capital) and owner's equity, which won't turn to cash until and unless the business is sold.

A glossary containing definitions of the terms used in the balance sheet is provided in the Appendix, page 147.

Filling in your balance sheet is easy once you know what all the terms mean. No mathematics more complex than addition and subtraction is involved. What you are trying to find out is how your business measures up against other businesses and how your assets and liabilities are distributed.

Depreciation and amortisation are technicalities best left to your accountant. They affect asset values by writing their purchase and installation costs off as expenses over the expected life of the asset according to some rather arbitrary tax codes. Ask your accountant to help you.

Using the balance sheet

Comparing one business with another using balance sheets is always informative.

Comparing one business with another using balance sheets is always informative. For start-ups, comparisons are particularly valuable. You must have a good reason to depart from the average distribution of assets and liabilities. This doesn't mean you have to model your balance sheet on the norm. Start with how you want your business to be shaped, check to see how others have done it, then make changes that may be suggested by those other businesses. They represent experience, while you represent hope. Keep the two in some kind of tension, and you'll do better than going to either extreme (of slavishly copying the average, or blundering heedlessly ahead on whim).

Once you have been in business for a while, looking for changes in the balance sheet can be instructive. A balance sheet is a picture of the business at a given time, so changes are inevitable. Look for changes in debt and in current assets first, then compare other areas.

Working Capital: The difference between Current Assets and Current Liabilities is called Working Capital. The amount of working capital available is a good measure of your ability to meet current obligations and will be examined by your banker when you apply for a loan. Having adequate working capital is a necessity for long-term survival.

Three ratios, which can be quickly calculated from figures on your balance sheet, are particularly useful. They are:

Current Ratio: Divide Current Assets by Current Liabilities to determine your business's liquidity (ability to meet current obligations).

Quick or Acid Test: Divide Cash and Sales ledger by Current Liabilities. Since Sales ledger figures are close to cash, this is a better measure of liquidity (in some ways) than the Current Ratio.

Debt-to-Worth Ratio: Divide Total Liabilities by Net Worth. Many banks look at this to determine how much risk the owner should shoulder.

Secure the necessary financing

Most start-ups rely on the owner's capital to encourage the bank to lend more money. If you can avoid borrowing, by all means do so. But you will be a rare bird indeed. You may want to take out a bank loan anyway, to prepare for future growth needs. Banks like to have credit experience with borrowers before lending substantial sums, so a small loan repaid on time can pave the way for obtaining greater sums in the future.

If you can avoid borrowing, you will be a rare bird indeed.

The assumption, however, is that you will go where all small businesses go sooner or later: to the bank to raise some cash.

Before you visit your bank manager, make sure that your balance sheet, sales forecast, and cash flow projection are updated and thoroughly documented. Credibility with your banker is a great asset, but one that is hard to gain and easily impaired. Since your balance sheet and cash flow have been prepared on the basis of your research and plans for your business, you have to be the person to talk to your bank manager. Bring along your financial adviser if you wish, but be prepared to answer most of the questions yourself. ('Why do you think this sales level will be reached? What if it isn't?')

You may find that you need either collateral or a co-signatory. Banks like collateral because it shows that you are committed to the success of your business and won't walk away from it if things get rough. A co-signatory can provide a depth of collateral that satisfies the important bankerly concern about the security of the loans they make. Some possibilities for raising finance are:

- Fixed-term loan from your bank.
- Bank overdraft.
- Government loan guarantee scheme. As 70 per cent of the loan (up to £100,000 for two to seven years) is guaranteed by the Department of Employment, banks are encouraged to lend to new businesses and those which cannot meet the normally stringent demands for security.
- Business loan from local development agencies; the Rural Development Commission in small English towns; British Steel Corporation and British Coal Enterprise in areas affected by steel and mining closures.

Use your cash flow forecast and your balance sheet
This is where your cash flow projection and balance sheet are invaluable. There is no better way to demonstrate competence and commitment to your bank or other financing source than to present a clear, well-documented set of financial statements.

As noted above, your cash flow will show you the amount of capital that you need. If you have had the foresight to keep your bank involved from early on in the cash flow forecast process, this will be simple. If not, the cash flow will provide an excellent framework to discuss your real financing needs. The balance sheet will have to be revised after you secure finance, but that's a trivial task. At this stage, the balance sheet shows how the assets and liabilities add up.

- How much debt should you take on?
- What kind of debt makes the most sense?
- What will your borrowing requirements be in six months? In a

year? Your long-term goals come into play when you discuss basic capitalisation. Your bank manager can (and will) help you to think through these needs.

If the response is that you are undercapitalised, get more capital. If you can't, don't start your business until you have adequate capital.

Bank managers are conservative. They have to be. Their advice is based on working with many small businesses, and if you disagree with their advice they should be able to explain their position to your satisfaction. Remember that it is in your mutual interests to determine the most sensible debt structure for your business. If your bank manager suggests a different structure than you had planned on, listen to him or her. You will learn something that will help you ultimately, even if you end up looking for another bank or bank manager.

Bank managers are conservative. They have to be.

If you intend to accept credit cards, make arrangements now

You may yourself want to offer credit to your customers, but credit is an area that takes a lot of skill. Credit cards are a good way of shifting the burden of assessing creditworthiness and collecting cash to organisations that know how. The cost will range from 1.5 to 7 per cent depending on your business, your bank's experience and the amounts involved. Most businesses find that the average sale is sufficiently higher when credit cards are used to warrant the bank's discount.

Open bank accounts

Banks are in business to make money by lending out their depositors' money. If you plan to use a bank's credit services (loans, credit cards, etc), offer them your deposit business while negotiating your loan or credit card. They can tell you what kind of deposit services make sense for you, and as banking becomes increasingly competitive, will probably insist that you bank with them if you borrow from them.

Secure insurance cover

Select your business insurance agent with the same care with which you chose your solicitor, bank manager and accountant. Since this area calls for professional expertise, think carefully whether your friendly life assurance agent has the skills to handle your business requirements.

Select your business insurance agent with the same care with which you chose your solicitor, bank manager and accountant.

93

Insurance is a necessity. You are legally required to provide certain cover (for example motor vehicle, employer's liability for death, injury or disease to employees caused in the course of employment). Depending on your business, other cover may be mandatory (for example, solicitors, riding establishments, merchant shippers).

Some trade organisations offer an insurance package to their members which will include all the essentials.

As the owner of a small business, make sure that you are protected against the normal business hazards: fire, theft, flood, accident, etc.

Use of land and buildings

Check that your proposed use of the building complies with local planning; this is likely to be relevant if you wish to change the use to which a building has been put, in which case planning permission will be required. Contact your Borough or District Council Planning Department.

Determine image, advertising, promotion and public relations strategies

Put your customers first. How will they perceive your products and services?

Sources of low-cost help in determining how best to represent your business include TEC and Small Firms Service counsellors. You can also ask other business owners who they use: this is often the best way to locate capable local marketing help. Big advertising agencies aren't interested in small budgets, but local agencies are often interested in locating clients to grow with. The smaller agencies (including public relations and marketing consultants) are usually the best bet for start-up businesses, although you will have to pay for their expertise.

The ideal case is where the expert becomes a part of your management team.

As before: shop around to find the right marketing help for you and your business. The ideal case is where the expert becomes a part of your management team, helps you to save money by sparing you the expense of learning to do it yourself, and most important of all, helps to ensure that your promotional efforts (advertising of all sorts, public relations and any other promotional efforts including grand openings) are targeted to the right people through the right media for your business.

This presupposes that a lot of work has already been done on your part. You know whom you want to reach, you know what their interests are apt to be and what benefits you can offer them – and what you can afford to spend in your marketing efforts. A general word of caution: make sure you budget sufficiently for two kinds of promotional activity. The first is the ongoing campaign to keep your name in your customers' eye – usually through the local media (newspaper, Yellow Pages, perhaps radio or cable TV). The second is for special events, opportunities or challenges such as sudden intense competition.

Use outside experts

The dangers of do-it-yourself promotions, or of using inexperienced people, are that you put out the wrong message to the wrong people at the wrong time through the wrong media. If any one of these areas is bungled (message, market, timing or media) you are throwing money away. Advertising that fails to achieve any positive goal is expensive, no matter how little cash you spend on it. Talk to advertising agencies and other experts. Use your advisers to corroborate your instincts or back up your decisions – but be prepared to pay for marketing and promotional skills. Once you know what you are doing you may be able to bring some of this effort back in-house, but for a start-up, don't even think of cutting corners here. It won't work.

Advertising that fails to achieve any positive goal is expensive, no matter how little cash you spend on it.

Recheck logo and name of business

Once you have some promotional help, go over the name of your business, your logo and other materials that help to project your image to your public with the experts. Sometimes very subtle changes can make a big difference. You may not be tuned in to the effect of different typefaces, or colours, or the implications of a name, but these can be important. Even big companies have been known to mess this one up. Chevrolet vigorously promoted their Nova model in Spanish-speaking countries before discovering to their chagrin that *No va* means 'doesn't go'. Hardly an endorsement for a car!

Establish promotion and advertising plans

Solicit help from your advertising agent or other promotional experts on your grand opening strategy. It doesn't matter whether you're opening a professional practice or a retail store. Start-ups have an advantage (they are new) and a disadvantage (nobody knows about them). How you deal with opening promotions can make a substantial difference in the first few months of your business.

If you plan a celebration, line up the caterer or the musicians or whatever now, well in advance of the opening. If you plan a media event, plan ahead.

You may be able to garner some publicity (business openings are news), but to make sure of the best timing and placement, give the editor a lead time of six weeks or so; trade publications usually require even more lead time, while local papers and radio stations need less. Ask your promotion specialist for advice on putting together press releases. It's an art that you can learn, but you don't want to waste the edge that being new gives you.

You also want to make sure the medium you choose is appropriate. For instance, if your product or service is truly innovative, don't spend too much time on your local paper or radio station. Look for editors and producers who can spread your news further afield.

Order professionally designed stationery, signboards, etc

The danger of sending out printed materials with the wrong image can be minimised by getting a graphic artist to design your stationery, invoices, business cards, invitations, etc. The cost is minimal, the benefits long-lasting.

Order opening stock

Make sure you order your opening stock in plenty of time to get it in for start-up. If you run into a situation where you face a long order cycle, you may be better off postponing opening until such time as you have adequate stock. Nothing looks quite as foolish as empty shelves (unless you are in the empty shelf business, like Hannah).

Nothing looks quite as foolish as empty shelves.

Complete improvements to your premises

Extensive alterations, painting and carpeting take time. The earlier you can pin down your contractor (or allocate some of your own time if you plan to do it yourself) the better. Ideally, these jobs will be completed 30 to 60 days before opening to give you time to alter things that don't look or feel right and to make sure that those special lights you ordered actually arrive.

Some improvements that are occasionally overlooked include:

- office walls
- special lighting fixtures
- heating/ventilation/air conditioning
- display areas: shelving, carpeting, display windows
- storage areas
- point-of-sale displays
- security improvements: alarms, shutters, lights.

Start recruiting

If you need to recruit staff, start now. Sixty days is usually long enough to allow for taking on the right person.

Use job descriptions

A job description outlines the skills, education and experience required for the job you wish to fill. A form is provided in the Appendix, page 131.

Job descriptions are extremely valuable personnel tools. Writing a job description makes you pay attention to the job (Is it needed at all? What are the characteristics of a good applicant?) and avoid the pitfalls of discrimination. Yes, you can be selective: you don't have to recruit anyone you don't feel is both willing and able to do the job. Discrimination problems arise when different standards are applied on the basis of race, gender, or other criteria.

Job descriptions also help you to determine wage ranges, recruit from a pool of possible employees, and to communicate with your employees once they have started working for you. A job description doesn't have to tie your hands ('It's not in my job description' doesn't have a role in small business), but it does help to make clear what a job involves, what its responsibilities and duties are.

Choose from more than three applicants

If you have fewer than three qualified applicants for a job, you run a very high risk of making a poor recruiting decision.

Three is an arbitrary number, but if you have fewer than three qualified applicants for a job, you run a very high risk of making a poor recruiting decision. Newspaper ads, employment agencies, Jobcentres, college noticeboards, word of mouth and time provide enough candidates to help make good recruiting decisions.

Arrange interviews

Since you have to juggle a lot of balls at this time, fitting interviews in becomes a problem. Don't depend on help appearing off the street. Set interview schedules and stick to them. Taking on staff is the biggest problem area for many business owners. A mistake is very costly (in terms of time and money), but recruiting is not something that many people have experience of. Interviews are even worse: it's easy to jump at the first good applicant. Don't! Try to find an appropriate seminar or workshop and take it. And, most important, remember to check your applicants' references.

Inform your local tax office.

Get in touch with your local tax office

It is necessary to inform your local Inspector of Taxes that you are starting up. When you take on staff, ask for a starter pack that will contain all the information you need to operate Pay As You Earn (PAYE) and National Insurance contributions (NICs).

Refine your mission statement

Go back to your mission statement. Does it still fit? Does it feel right? Does it express what your business should become? You will have increasing reasons to have a clear mission statement in the next few weeks. Set some time aside to review it with your advisers. Even if your decision is to stick with the statement you already have, it is time well spent.

You can use your mission statement as a guide to making decisions. If a proposed action doesn't further the accomplishment of the mission, question whether or not that action should be performed. Usually it shouldn't be.

A case study (continued)

Hannah's balance sheet

Line 6: Cash. This is Hannah's initial investment, currently in a bank ready for her to use.

Line 7: Commissions due. Doesn't apply at start-up, but will next year. She makes the sale, collects commissions over a period of months. See cash inflows on the cash flow projection.

Line 8: Prepaid expenses. Hannah anticipated and paid sizable consulting and professional fees before start-up. This ensures continuity of professional advice.

Line 9: Stock. Needed for initial sales efforts.

Line 10: Supplies. Not applicable at this time.

Line 15: Office equipment. Old typewriter, cabinet, desk.

Line 17: Car. Hannah's car, put in company's name to simplify some tax planning on the advice of her accountant.

Line 26: Bought ledger. Current portion of balance due on car, training sessions, dues, and subscriptions.

Line 30: Long-term liabilities. Remainder of car loan.

Hannah's start-up balance sheet isn't as useful a tool as it will be in a few months or a year. After being in business for a while, her balance sheet will more closely resemble those of other sales reps in her kind of business. It is important, however, to keep the balance sheet straight from the start. It forms part of the tax record, helps to measure progress, and provides a fixed point for comparison with other businesses.

Hannah's Balance Sheet

	D	A	B	C	D
1		31 December, 19XX			
2					
3		ASSETS			
4					
5		CURRENT ASSETS			
6	15,000	Cash			15,000
7	0	Commissions due			0
8	5,000	Prepaid expenses			5,000
9	1,000	Stock			1,000
10	0	Supplies			0
11	21,000	TOTAL CURRENT ASSETS:			21,000
12					
13		FIXED ASSETS (net of depreciation)			
14	0	Display material			0
15	750	Office equipment			750
16	0	Leasehold improvements			0
17	4,500	Car			4,500
18	5,250	TOTAL FIXED ASSETS:			5,250
19					
20	26,250	TOTAL ASSETS:			26,250
21					
22		LIABILITIES & NET WORTH			
23					
24		CURRENT LIABILITIES:			
25	0	Taxes due			0
26	4,500	Bought ledger			4,500
27					
28	4,500	TOTAL CURRENT LIABILITIES:			4,500
29					
30	3,000	LONG TERM LIABILITIES:			3,000
31					
32					
33	3,000	TOTAL LONG TERM LIABILITIES:			3,000
34					
35	7,500	TOTAL LIABILITIES:			7,500
36					
37	18,750	NET WORTH:			18,750
38					
39	26,250	TOTAL LIABILITIES & NET WORTH:			26,250

Action Plan

Objective	Action/Strategy	Target date	Person responsible	Results/Comments
Prepare marketing plan	Refine mission statement (ongoing)			
	Maintain competitor files (ongoing)			
	Review non-financial objectives (2 weeks)			
	Review sales forecast (2 weeks)			
	Determine image, PR, other promotion plans			
Prepare balance sheet	Consult financial adviser			
Establish bank relationship and secure financing	Set up an appointment with bank manager (10 days)			
	Update cash flow (immediate)			
	Open bank accounts			
	Make arrangements for accepting credit cards			
	Meet insurance agent to secure insurance cover (within 10 days)			
	Meet solicitor for review			
Prepare for opening	Order opening stock (immediate)			
	Establish advertising and promotion plans			
	Schedule improvements to premises (within 10 days)			
	Complete improvements (within 45 Days)			

Objective	Action/Strategy	Target date	Person responsible	Results/Comments
Start hiring the right people	Prepare job descriptions (within 10 days)			
	Seek applicants; place ads (10–45 days)			
	Begin recruiting, training (asap)			

◀ CHAPTER 7 ▶

ONE MONTH BEFORE START-UP

It takes at least a month to get the final details thoroughly nailed down. Something will crop up unexpectedly; deliveries won't be made; improvements to the premises will take longer than planned; some legal hitch will surface. Count on it.

How can you ensure that your business opening will be smooth?

The checklist approach is a start. Make a long list of what has to be done, then work backwards to see when you should start doing each item. Allow extra time, since schedules always run over. Your aim is to have a trouble-free opening. In business, as in any enterprise, well begun is half finished. Get off to the best start you can.

In business, as in any enterprise, well begun is half finished.

Fine tune your cash flow budget

You will find that your budget needs a certain amount of tinkering on a steady basis, especially during the start-up months when experience begins to correct assumptions. Don't allow yourself to be paralysed by aiming for perfection in your budgeting. Budgeting is a difficult art and science to master. You'll improve with time.

Check your sales forecast *again*. Most disbursements are predictable (within limits). The biggest variable to worry about is cash from operations. You can be more definite about cash from new loans or capital, and at this stage cash from sale of fixed assets isn't likely. A common pattern for many start-up retail businesses is a flurry of activity (due to start-up publicity and natural local curiosity) followed by a slump that may last any time from two to six months as a steady repeat customer base develops.

As a general rule, the conservative approach to cash flow is best. Expect revenue to develop slowly. Expect expenditure to grow faster than you plan. The cushion of working capital you build into your financing should see you through this period.

Set up variance reports

Variance reports (see the sample in the Appendix, page 134) help you to keep track of actual against budgeted performance on a monthly basis. Your accountant or other financial advisers will help you to set this up for your business. If there is a sizeable variation in any budgeted item, look into it. It may turn up a problem or an oppportunity, and in either event, the sooner you are aware of what is going on the better. As an example, if telephone costs are much below what you expected, it could mean that the bill wasn't paid, or that you aren't using the phone the way you planned, or that you over-budgeted. The point is that if you are aware of such deviations, you can make informed decisions and profit.

The variance report also forces you to refer to your budget at least once a month. A surprising number of business owners don't use a budget (or don't have one), and as a result run out of cash. Don't be one of them.

You may wish to keep track of some variables such as sales and cash position on a weekly or even daily basis. Mapping this information (using a graph with cash on the vertical line, dates on the horizontal line) can be extremely informative over a period. (A computer makes this easy to do.) The cumulative impact of this kind of information is hard to beat.

You may want to follow some non-financial variables that will affect your business. Chargeable hours, new customer or prospect contacts, and call reports for salespeople are examples.

The aim of these reports is not to drown you in paperwork (many of them take only a few minutes to prepare), but to make managing your new enterprise easier. In a going concern, established routines and experience are often substitutes for these reports (and are not usually adequate substitutes). As the new business in the area, if you do more things right than your competitors do, you'll get off to a good start.

Prepare for your grand opening

Plan ahead and be prepared. Whatever can go wrong, will.

Whether you are planning a retail or service business, an opening ceremony of some kind is in order. You can get local press coverage free; you gain an immediate presence in the community; and you get an invaluable chance to control the first impression your business makes.

Whether you are planning a retail or service business, an opening ceremony of some kind is in order.

You don't have to invest in marching bands and fancy balloons. A grand opening can be anything from announcements through the post to a circus, depending on what image you are trying to present. Shops often use a sale (Special Opening Offer!) or have some special featured item to make their statement to their customers.

Since this will be your first opportunity to publicise your start-up, make the best of it. Use your advisers. Ask your advertising agency or marketing consultant to help you think it through. You only have one shot at this, so don't waste it.

Rehearse

A grand opening is first cousin to a theatrical performance. You have to make sure that the premises are clean, shelves stocked, office equipped and personnel trained for the event. If you are still hiring staff the day you open the doors for business, make sure the new workers understand that they will be making first impressions that affect the future of your business and their jobs.

- If you plan to use caterers or other outside help for the event, make sure they are lined up at least 30 days in advance, then check with them a week before the event to make sure they still plan to be there. Go over the schedules and instructions the day before the event, and make sure they plan to arrive in plenty of time to set up and get ready.
- Order flowers or other decorations a week early.
- Schedule grand opening hours. People need to know when to come and when to leave.

- Have co-ordinated advertising material ready (brochures, business cards, price-lists or other handout material with the business's name, address, phone number and logo on it). Make sure your printer is aware of your deadline. You might want to set it two weeks before the opening date. If the job needs to be changed or redone, you'll still be on schedule.
- Invite the local press 30 days ahead of time, with a follow-up invitation a week before the event. Make sure they receive whatever press release your advertising or marketing advisers recommend.
- Local politicians love to be photographed helping new businesses to get started. Invite them.
- Follow up. For instance, a guest book for people to sign and leave their addresses in can become the basis for a mailing list. A 'three-month-(or one-year)-after-opening' story may interest your local paper.

Local politicians love to be photographed helping new businesses to get started. Invite them.

Your grand opening is a marketing opportunity. Seize it.

Set up your office, display areas, etc

At least 15 days before you open, set up your office and display areas. This gives you some time to shift things about and make the place feel right before you get caught up in the maelstrom of opening. The more of this kind of tinkering you can do before opening the better: it keeps you busy. Many people find that once start-up is in sight they get impatient and fretful, and having some physical, immediately rewarding activities connected with the business is a great help.

Do your final professional check

About two weeks before opening, ask your professional advisers for a final check.

The less you have to worry about the better. About two weeks before opening, ask your professional advisers (solicitor, accountant, insurance agent, or other consultant) for a final check.

- Ask your solicitor to check that any necessary licences have been acquired and other legal odds and ends have been attended to. One reason you need a solicitor familiar with small business practices is that these checks are routine, and he or she can perform them quickly, thoroughly and inexpensively. While you could save a few pounds by doing them yourself, the risk isn't worth the saving.

- Ask your accountant or other financial adviser to review your bookkeeping set-up, basic record-keeping system, and compliance with tax requirements. There may be last-minute changes or adjustments that will serve you well. If not, you know that things are in order and ready to go.

- Is all legally required insurance cover satisfied, and the optional cover you and your insurance adviser have decided upon taken out? Careful attention to these small details now can save you big worries later. Arrange for an insurance review on at least an annual basis; this is the first.

Arrange for an insurance review on at least an annual basis.

- Ask your marketing and other consultants, formal or informal, to go over your opening strategy, operating plans and financing with you. At this late date you may not be able to effect any big changes before opening, but if you have been careful, this session will provide a lot of reassurance. It can also plug some small gaps. Anything you can do to improve the odds of success is worth doing.

Engage your staff

Engaging staff is a tricky business. You don't want to pay out wages if it isn't necessary, yet you may have to take on and train your employees before start-up. Last month you began the recruiting and interviewing process, and may have made some recruiting decisions. This month, the problem is engaging people (including negotiating wages), getting those people up to scratch, and preparing them for the opening.

Remuneration packages

Broadly interpreted, remuneration packages include salary or wages, working conditions, opportunities for advancement, fringe benefits, training and even a social component. As a small business owner you have some latitude in what you offer to make your business attractive to employees, but you can't compete directly with a large company in terms of pay or benefits.

You can compete effectively in terms of offering an interesting, varied, concerned and convenient working environment. A few guidelines are:

- **Use pay scales.** As a rule, you get what you pay for. Local pay scales can be established by questioning other business owners, keeping track of job ads, checking with the local Jobcentre, and even by asking employment agencies. Sometimes large businesses in your area will divulge information about rates of pay. A pay scale for each job should set a bottom and top figure. Within that range, wages will vary according to the experience of the applicant, your needs, availability of labour and a number of other factors. Offering more than other businesses won't necessarily get you the best applicants and will set a precedent that's hard to maintain. It will get you the hungriest applicants, who will stick with you only until a better offer comes along (and it will).

- **Provide training.** If you used job descriptions in the hiring process, spotting areas where additional training is needed will be simplified. Training, especially sales training, has such a fast, high return that not providing it is a foolish economy. More importantly, offering training shows employees that you are interested in their development. Good employees appreciate the chance to improve their skills. You benefit from better employees; they benefit from the chance to get ahead. Gaining a reputation as a good trainer is a powerful long-term employment strategy.

Gaining a reputation as a good trainer is a powerful long-term employment strategy.

- **Offer employee benefits.** You can offer flexible hours, job sharing, or other benefits that don't cost much but are important to your employees. Possible fringe benefits range from holiday pay to education and training, insurance and pension schemes to child care and sick leave. Small businesses can be more flexible than big companies – an advantage for you.

Bear in mind that benefits once granted are hard to take back. What do other local employers offer? What are the costs? Can you make the benefits contingent on performance?

Know the importance of customer service

If you teach your employees one thing, teach them the following aphorism (invented by the owner of a large and successful supermarket): 'Rule one is that the customer is always right. Rule two is that if the customer is wrong, see rule one.' Customers *are* your business. They are your most valuable asset. And they are easily lost.

All employees should be trained in customer service from Day 1. Before start-up, this is even more important. You want to establish a reputation for putting the customer first if your business is to prosper.

- **Train all your employees to be courteous.** The role of common courtesy is often overlooked. Every study of former customers demonstrates this. The most common reason given for not going back to a shop or service provider is that the customer felt poorly treated. Have you ever stood at a counter while assistants discussed their private lives? Waited for over an hour for a solicitor to see you?

- **Make sure everyone knows the word-of-mouth fallacy.** The customer who feels poorly treated complains to an average of 11 other people. However, it is not true, as widely believed, that customers who receive courteous treatment tell others. If you remember that the secret of successful marketing is minimising the opportunities for customer dissatisfaction, courtesy training is an important marketing tactic.

- **'Coddle the customer'** because the customer makes your business. The customer pays the bills. The customer is boss. No customer – no business. And it costs roughly five times as much to acquire a new customer as to keep an old one. This is why Marks and Spencer cheerfully refunds money or replaces merchandise to its customers without quibbling. Upset a customer and you run the risk of losing 11 others. Treat that customer right, and you retain a friendly ambassador.

It costs roughly five times as much to acquire a new customer as to keep an old one.

Make sure everything works

Before opening, run through as many procedures as you can. Is everything in place, plugged in, ready to go? It is easier to correct minor hitches before you open than later.

Include security procedures

The Russian proverb 'trust, but verify' applies to business as well as to international relations.

- Who opens and closes the office or shop?
- Set up procedures for making sure the electric kettle is turned off, the alarms turned on, the doors locked and so on.

- Arrange for periodic security checks.
- Ask your accountant to review cash handling and other sensitive business procedures.

Implement marketing, promotion and opening plans

Congratulations! You are now in business.

Action Plan

Objective	Action/Strategy	Target date	Person responsible	Results/Comments
Make sure all systems are working	Fine tune financial statements (10 days)			
	Set up office, display, sales area (10 days)			
	Make final legal and licensing check (10 days)			
	Check all utilities, improvements, etc (20 days)			
Complete personnel preparation	Hire necessary staff (asap)			
	Provide training for courtesy, customer-centred sales (ongoing)			
Get ready for opening	Send announcements (14 days)			
	Implement promotion plans (asap)			

◄ CHAPTER 8 ►

START-UP AND AFTER

Don't change your plans without good reasons.

In the first few months your business is in operation, you will be busier than you have ever been or ever will be again. The key to getting through these months successfully is: stick to your objectives. You spent months deciding what your business is, who your markets are, and what (and why) they will buy from you. You decided what promotions made sense, what kind of image to project, and what to do if things didn't go exactly as planned.

Under the pressure of daily business, with experience correcting your forecasts (often in a negative way), it becomes very tempting to try to do a little more, add a product or service, go after a different market, buy market share, or any of thousands of possible responses to outside forces. Be stalwart. Stick to your plan for three months. That gives you enough time (in most cases) to get over the initial excitement of running your own business, meet the wage bill and other fixed expenses several times, and get a better grip on what your business patterns will actually be.

Stick to your plan for three months.

Initially, sales may be higher than anticipated followed by a substantially lower sales pattern than hoped for. This is a common pattern and doesn't mean that your plans were off mark. Initial sales often come from the newness factor, and after the novelty for your customers wears off, sales will build slowly in a more normal pattern. Assuming that you did your homework in the pre-start-up period, these swings will even out.

Some ways of keeping your enthusiasm high include organising your time effectively (that is, doing the right things at the right times), updating your product/benefit list from your customers' viewpoint, and paying extra attention to communications with your markets. Expect to make mistakes – you're human. But plan to learn from your mistakes (and from your successes). You will learn more about your business in the first three to six months than you will in the next five years. That's exhilarating.

You will learn more about your business in the first three to six months than you will in the next five years.

Manage your time

Within the first month of operation you'll find certain habits and patterns emerging: you go to work, open the door, and how do you spend your time? Time is a finite – and precious – resource, and your best investment is managing your own time to make sure you don't leave any major aspect of your business undernourished. In successful businesses every important management area is given adequate attention. Unsuccessful businesses are lop-sided. We all prefer to spend time doing things we enjoy, and try to avoid (if possible) those tasks we dislike. This poses a simple choice: either manage your time to avoid those gaps, or don't manage your time and wake up in a sweat at 3.00 am wondering if you remembered to fill in that tax form or make that loan payment.

When managing your time, keep these points in mind:

- The tasks of management are: to plan, coordinate, direct, control, monitor, evaluate, correct, review and innovate. These areas require attention on a regular basis.

- Set aside time for your family and for yourself to avoid burnout. The temptation to spend all your time at work is beguiling, but the costs in personal terms are excessive. Build in some time for yourself as well. Getting away from the hurly burly of business pays off and results in better judgement and making better decisions.

Set aside time to get to know your customers better.

- Set aside time for learning more about your business (information pays). You can never know too much about your business, the industry it's in, and general management and economic issues.

112

- Set aside time to get to know your customers better. Talk to them. Ask them questions; listen to their answers. There's a good reason for the fact that you have two ears and one tongue. Listen twice as much as you talk, and you'll become wise. Make sure to get as many customers' names, addresses and information about their interests and preferences as possible for marketing purposes.

- Set aside time to research your competition. The more you know about your competition, both direct and indirect, the better. Maintain those competitor files religiously. Check out your competition. Speak to their customers and suppliers. They act as a mirror for your own business's improvements.

Continuously update your products/service

This is where your interests and those of your customers intersect. If you remain attuned to their wants and preferences and shape your product or service to their needs, you win. If you try to force what you happen to have to sell on a public that doesn't want to buy, you're in deep trouble.

Listen

- To customers
- To your family and friends
- To your employees
- To suppliers
- To competitors
- To advisers

And listen to yourself. People like to give advice. Your role as business owner is to listen, *evaluate* what you hear, and act accordingly, based on your judgement and experience. This is not a recommendation that you weigh every bit of input equally. You learn from others, selectively, by applying the intelligence and experience that urged you to go into business on your own in the first place.

Your role as business owner is to listen, *evaluate* what you hear, and act accordingly.

Check cash flow budget against actual performance

The budget imposes a discipline that is especially important when you are in the early stages of operation and money is tight. 'If in doubt, do without' isn't a bad motto, especially when you're backed up by a cash flow budget that shows what you can and cannot afford to do.

Ask your accountant to set up a variance analysis program to follow. In variance analysis, you compare, line item by line item, actual to projected performance. Your cash flow budget is a projected set of figures; actual performance will differ, but usually not drastically. By faithfully comparing these two sets of figures monthly (or more often), you accomplish two important objectives: you become aware of exactly what is going on financially in your business, and you learn what those changing numbers reveal about operations. Financial statements used properly have great power.

Update your plans as needed

Losing sight of objectives is the biggest danger small business owners run.

The main thrust of your plan should not change.

Plan your business carefully, follow your plan, and make adjustments only if necessary. The main thrust of your plan, as embodied in your mission statement and long-term objectives, should not change. The urge to change it to take advantage of an opportunity or add some cash to the till is hard to resist.

Before making any radical changes in what your business does, check with your advisory board, discuss the proposed actions with your counsellors, and make sure your bank manager is alerted.

Maintain good communications with your bank manager and suppliers

The basic rule for dealing with your bank manager, suppliers and investors is simply the golden rule: Do unto others as you would like other to do unto you. It's good business. Treat them the way you like to be treated: honestly, fairly and consistently.

Working with your bank manager

The primary source of money for your small business will be your bank. Accordingly, you have to choose and nurture a bank manager. Your relationship with your bank manager has to be based on factual information as well as on some intangibles, but above all bear in mind that bank managers do not like surprises. Keep him or her informed of bad news as well as good, and of any major changes in the way you do business. The results will be worth the effort.

Bank managers have to be satisfied on two key questions:

1. Does this loan make sense for the business?
2. How will the loan be repaid? If things don't work out, what is the secondary repayment source?

Some common misconceptions about banks are that they will only lend you money when you don't need it, that they are insensitive to start-ups (and small businesses in general), and that they want to own your house and other possessions. Unprepared applicants seldom get the financing they think they deserve; people expect the bank to whittle down their loan requests, so they ask for far too much in the first place, which destroys their credibility from the outset.

Matching the term of your loan to your financing

Your bank will match the financing with the reason for the financing. A bank manager's rule of thumb is *never borrow short term to meet a long-term obligation, and never borrow long term to cover a short-term obligation.*

- Short-term loans are used for short-term needs: loans to cover stocking with repayment to come from selling the stock are usually 30–90 days. A straightforward overdraft facility might suffice: you overdraw up to the agreed limit and pay interest only on the overdraft that you take up. On a short-term loan, you pay interest on the whole period of the total borrowing. (Chronic cash flow shortages reflect undercapitalisation or poor cash management. Both are serious problems that your bank manager will want you to solve as soon as possible.)

- Equipment loans are repaid from operating profits over a period not to exceed the life of the equipment. These are usually set up as term loans, with fixed payments made on a regular working basis, over one to seven years. Working capital loans are treated the same way. Such loans are often arranged by the company selling the equipment.

- Mortgages are long-term loans used to purchase property and may extend up to 15 or 20 years.

Bankers always want their small business customers to become bigger businesses.

Ask your bank manager for help, explaining that your plans and your cash flow indicate your need for a loan. Put the bank manager in your team. Your bank manager is experienced in financial areas that you are not (he or she will see 200 or more business loan applications each year) and has a vested interest in seeing you succeed. Bankers always want their small business customers to become bigger businesses.

Banks are not venture capitalists or charitable organisations. They make their profit by investing their depositors' money. They can't make a profit if they don't get the money back, so they are conservative, avoid risky ventures and long shots.

Bankers have been trained in observing the five Cs of credit for many years. Become aware of their concerns and you will have a better probability of securing the kind of financing that will help your business grow (and grow profitably).

The five Cs of credit

Loans to small businesses are not normal commercial loans in the sense that they are made to individuals, not to businesses.

1. Character. Loans to small businesses are not normal commercial loans in the sense that they are made to individuals, not to businesses. Many bankers claim that in fact they never lend to small businesses, but rather are investing in the owner on the basis of knowing that person's character. Ultimately, the owner will be responsible for repayment of loans. You will find that you have to sign personally as a guarantor of any bank loan your business secures. The kind of person you are has a lot to do with the kind of reception you will get at the local bank. If you have a reputation for being honest, straightforward and responsible, you are more likely to get your loan application approved.

2. Credit. Your credit history is a key piece of the puzzle for your bank manager. How have you handled credit in the past? If you have paid your debts more or less on time, don't have a history of bankruptcy or county court proceedings, and have proved that you can use credit effectively, your banker will be somewhat reassured. A good credit record seldom causes the banker to make a loan, but a bad record will cause him or her to withdraw credit.

3. Capacity. How much debt can you safely take on, and how much can your business bear? Remember that small business loans tend to be made on the basis of the individual's ability to support that debt rather than on the strength of the business's cash flow. A careful cash flow projection will shift much of the burden to the business, but your bank will still look to you as the ultimate source of repayment. Your bank manager will ask for a personal financial statement as well as your business's balance sheet and cash flow in order to work out how much you can afford to borrow. He is the expert, so listen to him. He doesn't want to burden you with too much debt because he wants you to succeed.

4. Capital. You have to have at least as much at risk as the bank or other investors. This doesn't mean that your borrowing capacity is limited to what you can put in personally, but it does mean that you have to invest some of your own cash (plus, in some cases, the cash investment from other investors) in the deal. The 'creative financing, 100 per cent or 110 per cent leveraged deal' is not for business owners who plan to succeed. Your bank manager may ask you to secure more capital before a loan can be granted. Permanent capital (including subordinated debt) provides a cushion for the business and gives your bank a sense of security about lending you money.

5. Collateral. Your bank manager doesn't want to own your business or house or securities. He or she is in the banking business. Collateral is taken for two reasons: security (reduction of perceived risk to the bank) and commitment. Collateral represents a source of repayment in the worst case scenario (which reduces the risk of extending the credit in the first place). By putting up collateral, you show that you are at least as committed to the success of the venture as you expect the bank to be.

Collateral is taken for two reasons: security and commitment.

Working with your suppliers

Even though your bank will be the biggest single source of funds, your suppliers will (for most businesses) be your largest source of credit. Most small businesses purchase stock and services on credit and come to rely on their suppliers to bankroll them during periods of tight or negative cash flow.

You will find that you can't get much trade credit at first, but by punctilious payment of bills in small amounts, over time you will be able to enjoy customary trade credit. Remember that your suppliers are in business to make money and will respond the same way you do to evasive payment habits.

Make a list of suppliers and avoid becoming dependent on one or two. Shopping around is as good for your business as for your personal purchases, and it helps when times get tight.

If you hit a hard cash flow problem, be straight with your suppliers. Ask for their tolerance and you are more likely to receive it; they are aware that it costs about five times as much to get a new customer as to retain an old one, and they want you to make a go of your business. Small, consistent interim payments are a lot better than saying, 'The cheque is in the post,' 'I sent you the wrong cheque,' or 'The bookkeeper is on holiday and took the chequebook.'

Careful purchasing habits often provide all the profits for small retailers.

In more normal times, look closely at the terms of the sale. If your suppliers offer 2 per cent discount for payment in 10 days, net 30, and you can afford to take the discount, you'll earn about 36 per cent per year. This exceeds the rate you would pay to borrow from the bank. Ask your bank. Careful purchasing habits often provide all the profits for small retailers. Of course, you have to look at your cash flow, stock levels, and so on before making purchase and payment decisions.

Working with investors

Investors, like bankers, don't like surprises. If you have a drastic change in plan, or if your projections are thrown by unexpected competition, fire or theft or other major disaster, let them know. Fast. They want you to make a go of your business, and if kept informed will do their best to make your business succeed.

If something good happens, let them know. Fast. Don't save the good news for a time when you have to say 'Which do you want first, the good news or the bad?' They may be able to help you to capitalise on the good news, and will remember it when the news is bad.

Summary

Welcome to the club. Successful small businesses such as yours will be are not the result of good fortune. As golfer Arnold Palmer observed, 'The more I practise, the luckier I get.' Success (and luck) comes from hard work on the basics:

- Use information to balance your intuitions and hunches
- Place your customers' interests and concerns above all else
- Plan to meet those concerns profitably
- Implement your plan
- Adapt thoughtfully to change

To succeed and thrive, your business must grow in the direction and at the pace you feel is right for you and your business. You've already taken the steps that assure the maximum chance of success. Planning uses all your skills, both right-brained (creative and intuitive) and left-brained (analytic and reasoning). Your creative side will be constantly challenged as your business grows and economic and competitive climates change. The discipline imposed by your analytic side will channel that creativity and create the kind of business you deserve. Rely too heavily on either side and you'll act half-wittedly.

Have fun. One measure of small business success is the joy you bring to the job each day. Few activities are as exciting and challenging as making a small business prosper. The hard work you put in isn't drudgery. It's part of the pleasure of making your business really hum.

Few activities are as exciting and challenging as making a small business prosper.

And remember: you make your own luck. That is the best part of all. You (and you alone) control your future. Your income isn't dependent on a performance assessment and salary scale. Growth of your net worth isn't contingent on the vagaries of the stock market or a profit-sharing plan. You build your business – you reap the rewards.

Good luck. You'll make it work.

APPENDIX

APPENDIX

◀ APPENDIX 1 ▶

BUSINESS FORMS

The management audit

	Yes	*No*

1. We operate with a complete and up-to-date business plan, which includes:
1. Projections for at least three years ahead ☐ ☐
2. A capital budget ☐ ☐

2. The marketing plan is a major part of my business plan and includes:
1. The demographics of our market(s) ☐ ☐
2. A thoughtful definition of the market(s) we serve ☐ ☐
3. A definition of the need our products/services fill ☐ ☐
4. An analysis of the growth potential of our market(s) ☐ ☐
5. An analysis of the competition ☐ ☐
6. A description of what differentiates us from the competition ☐ ☐
7. Projections for other products/services that could be developed and timetables for research/development ☐ ☐

3. We use monthly budgets and statements which include:
1. Thorough and up-to-date records ☐ ☐
2. Variance analysis ☐ ☐
3. Itemised fixed and variable costs ☐ ☐
4. Standard cost comparisons ☐ ☐
5. Cash reconciliation ☐ ☐

Yes   *No*

4. We have developed an 'information base' which allows us to:
1. Keep track of new developments in the industry ☐ ☐
2. Obtain and study key trade information ☐ ☐
3. Understand what 'state-of-the-art' means in this business ☐ ☐
4. Provide customers with the best available information relating to our products/services ☐ ☐
5. Keep all our employees adequately informed ☐ ☐

5. I'm certain that the business is properly capitalised since I:
1. Base capitalisation on worst-case planning ☐ ☐
2. Have emergency funds or access to them ☐ ☐
3. Have discussed this with our bank ☐ ☐

6. I understand the value of the business because I've made use of:
1. Professionals in valuation ☐ ☐
2. Present value method to evaluate terms ☐ ☐
3. Professional tax planning counselling ☐ ☐

7. We strive to improve production, quality, and operations by:
1. Keeping the plant in top condition ☐ ☐
2. Maintaining safe conditions ☐ ☐
3. Establishing high standards ☐ ☐
4. Standing behind our products/services ☐ ☐
5. Not tolerating shoddy performance ☐ ☐
6. Working for consistency ☐ ☐
7. Using our company's 'look' as a statement to our customers ☐ ☐

8. Personnel decisions are based on humane, carefully considered policies, including:
1. Checklists to be sure objectives are clear ☐ ☐
2. Written job descriptions ☐ ☐
3. Regular progress and evaluation meetings ☐ ☐
4. Fair hiring practices ☐ ☐
5. Fair wage scales ☐ ☐

Yes   *No*

9. As for my own personal/managerial skills, I work hard to:

1. Develop my problem-solving skills ☐ ☐
2. Always stay calm ☐ ☐
3. Be objective ☐ ☐
4. Avoid investments in my own ego ☐ ☐
5. Listen to my employees ☐ ☐
6. Plan changes in our course to minimise negative effects ☐ ☐
7. Make decisions promptly ☐ ☐
8. Always get the facts behind problems ☐ ☐
9. Accept my own limitations ☐ ☐
10. Delegate tasks that can be done more efficiently by someone else ☐ ☐
11. Analyse all available options ☐ ☐
12. Develop my reading/study habits ☐ ☐
13. Improve my skills ☐ ☐
14. Consider risks ☐ ☐
15. Be positive with customers, employees, associates ☐ ☐

Personal data sheet

Name _____ Date of birth _____

Address _____

_____

Telephone number _____ Years there _____

Marital status _____ Name of spouse _____ Dependants _____

Education

	Name and address	Certificates/diplomas/degrees obtained
School		
College		
University		
Other		

Relevant training or work experience _____

_____

Work experience

Business and address	Job title and duties	Supervisor	Dates

Trade, professional or civic membership and activities _____

_____

Hobbies, interests, other relevant information _____

_____

_____

(*Use another sheet if necessary.*)

Credit enquiry

Name _____ Date of birth _____

Address _____

_____ Phone _____ Years there _____

Former address _____

Years there _____ Marital status _____ Name of spouse _____

No. of dependants (inc spouse) _____

Employer _____ Years there _____

Address _____

Phone _____ Kind of business _____

Position _____ Salary £ _____

Former employer and address _____ Years there _____

Spouse's employer and address _____

Salary £ _____ Other income sources – £/month _____

Account	Bank	A/c No.	Balance
Cheque			
Savings			

Car owned (year and make) _____ Purchased from _____ £_____

Financed by _____ Balance owed £ _____ Monthly _____

Rent or mortgage payment/month £ _____ Paid to _____

Property owned in name of _____ Purchase price _____ Mortgage bal _____

Credit references and all debts owing, other than above (Bank, finance companies)				
Name	Address	Orig amount	Balance	Monthly payment

Life assurance amount £ _____ Company _____

Nearest relative or friend not living with you/relationship _____

Address _____

Cost of living budget

(based on average month – does not cover purchase of any new items except emergency replacements)

Detailed budget

Regular monthly payments

£

House payments
(principal, interest, taxes, insurance) or rent

Car payments (including insurance)

Appliance, TV payments

Home improvement loan payments

Personal loan, credit card payments

Health plan payments

Life insurance premiums

Other insurance premiums

Savings/investments

Total

Household operating expenses

Telephone

Gas and electricity

Water

Other household expenses, repairs, maintenance

Total

Personal expenses

£

Clothing, cleaning, laundry

Doctor, dentist, optician

Education

Memberships

Gifts and contributions

Travel

Newspapers, magazines, books

Car maintenance and petrol

Spending money and allowances

Miscellaneous

Total

Food expenses

Food – at home

Food – away from home

Total

Taxes

Income tax

Community charge

National Insurance

Total

Budget summary

£

A. Gross income

Monthly total A _____

Less Expenses:

Regular monthly payments

Household operating expenses

Personal expenses

Food expenses

Tax

Monthly total B _____
_____

Savings (A–B) _____
_____

Job description form

Position _____

Date prepared _____

By _____

Task/Function	Estimated hours per week
1.	
2.	
3.	
4.	
5.	
6.	
7.	
8.	
9.	
10.	
Total hours	

Comments

Job description

Job specifications

Employee application form (Please print in block capitals)

Name _____ N.I. No. _____

Address _____

_____ Postcode _____

Telephone number _____ Date of birth ____/____/____

How did you hear of job? _____

School most recently attended:

Name _____ Address _____ Phone _____

Exams passed _____

_____

Three most recent jobs:

Company _____

Address _____ Phone _____

Job _____ Reporting to _____ Dates worked: from _____ to _____

Salary _____ Reason for leaving _____

_____

_____

Company _____

Address _____ Phone _____

Job _____ Reporting to _____ Dates worked: from _____ to _____

Salary _____ Reason for leaving _____

_____

_____

Company _____

Address _____ Phone _____

Job _____ Reporting to _____ Dates worked: from _____ to _____

Salary _____ Reason for leaving _____

_____

_____

Physical

Have you had any serious illnesses or do you have any physical handicaps?

If so, please give details _____

_____

What is your present state of health? _____

During the past 10 years have you ever been convicted of a crime, excluding misdemeanours and traffic violations? Yes _____ No _____ If yes, describe in full _____

_____

_____

(For jobs involving driving)

Do you hold a current UK driving licence? _____

Give dates and details of all convictions or impending prosecutions for motoring offences. If none, write 'None'.

Personal references (other than family)

Name _____ Telephone number _____

Name _____ Telephone number _____

Name _____ Telephone number _____

Interviewer or reference comments _____

_____

_____

_____

This section to be filled in only after engagement:

Job title _____ Hourly rate _____ Starting date ____/____/____

Person to contact in case of emergency _____

Phone number _____

I certify that the information contained in this application is correct to the best of my knowledge and understand that deliberate falsification of this information is grounds for dismissal.

Date _____ Signature _____

Variance report

From the Cash Flow Projection for the month of _____

	A Actual for month	B Budget for month	C Variance (B − A)	D % Variance (C/B × 100)
Opening Cash Balance				
Add:				
Cash Sales				
Sales ledger that has turned to Cash				
Other Cash Inflows				
Total Available Cash				
Deduct Estimated Disbursements:				
Cost of materials				
Variable labour				
Advertising				
Insurance				
Legal and accounting				
Delivery				
Equipment*				
Loan repayments				
Mortgage payment				
Rates				
Deduct Fixed Cash Disbursements:				
Utilities				
Salaries				
National Insurance				
Office supplies				
Maintenance and cleaning				
Licences				
Boxes, paper, etc				
Telephone				
Miscellaneous				
Total Disbursements				
Closing Cash Balance				

* Equipment expense represents actual expenditure for purchase of equipment

From the Income Statement for the month of _____

	A Actual for month	B Budget for month	C Variance (B−A)	D % Variance (C/B × 100)
Sales				
Less Cost of Goods				
Gross Profit on Sales				
Operating Expenses				
Variable Expenses Sales salaries (commissions) Advertising Miscellaneous variables				
Total Variable Expenses				
Fixed Expenses Utilities Salaries National Insurance Office supplies Insurance Maintenance and cleaning Legal and accounting Delivery Licences Boxes, paper, etc Telephone Miscellaneous Depreciation Interest				
Total Fixed Expenses				
Total Operating Expenses				
Net Profit (Gross Profit on Sales less Total Operating Expenses)				
Tax				
Net Profit After Taxes				

◀ APPENDIX 2 ▶

SOURCES OF FURTHER INFORMATION

The most useful texts available on small business start-up and management are listed below under the relevant chapter, together with names and addresses of organisations referred to in the text. The publications are all available from Kogan Page, unless the contrary is indicated.

Chapter 2: **One Year Before Start-Up**

The Entrepreneur's Complete Self-Assessment Guide, Douglas A Gray, 1989.

Which Business? Stephen Halliday, 2nd edition, 1990. Shows how to find business ideas and research their viability. Lists enterprise agencies and offices of the Rural Development Commission.

British Institute of Management
Management House, Cottingham Road, Corby, Northamptonshire NN17 1TT
0536 204222

Business in the Community
227a City Road, London EC1V 1LX
071-253 3716

Scottish Business in the Community
Romano House, 43 Station Road, Edinburgh EH12 7AF
031-334 9876

Business in the Community will be able to tell you your local Enterprise Agency.

Chambers of commerce

Association of British Chambers of Commerce
Sovereign House, 212a Shaftesbury Avenue, London WC2H 8EW
071-240 5831

Will be able to tell you your local chamber of commerce.

Department of Trade and Industry
1 Victoria Street, London SW1H 0ET
071-215 7877

For information relating to exporting, such as researching overseas markets.

Development boards

Enterprise Mid-Wales
Ladywell House, Newtown, Powys SY16 1JB
0686 26965

Highlands and Islands Development Board
Bridge House, 20 Bridge Street, Inverness IV1 1QR
0463 234171

Local Enterprise Development Unit
Lamont House, Purdy's Lane, Newtownbreda, Belfast BT8 4TB
0232 691031

Scottish Development Agency
Rosebery House, Haymarket Terrace, Edinburgh EH12 5EZ
031-337 9595

Industrial training boards
ITBs run courses and carry out research. They also have publications for sale.

Agricultural Training Board
32–34 Beckenham Road, Beckenham, Kent BR3 4PB
081-650 4890

Clothing and Allied Products Industry Training Board
80 Richardshaw Lane, Pudsey, Leeds LS28 6BN
0532 393355

Construction Industry Training Board
Dewhurst House, 24 West Smithfield, London EC1A 9JA
071-489 1662

Engineering Industry Training Board
PO Box 176, 54 Clarendon Road, Watford WD1 1LB
0923 38441

Hotel and Catering Industry Training Board
International House, High Street, London W5 5DB
081-579 2400

Man Made Fibres Industry Training Advisory Board
40 High Street, Rickmansworth, Hertfordshire WD3 1ER
0923 778371

Plastics Processing Industry Training Board
Coppice House, Halesfield 7, Telford, Shropshire TF7 4NA
0952 587020

Road Transport Industry Training Board
Capitol House, Empire Way, Wembley, Middlesex HA9 0NG
081-902 8880

Open College
Freepost TK1006, Brentford, Middlesex TW8 8BR
081-847 7788
Offers courses on business and office skills and running your own business, by distance learning.

Open University
Central Enquiry Service, PO Box 71, Milton Keynes MK7 6AG
Offers courses on business and management, and on business start-ups, by distance learning.

Pickup (Professional, Industrial and Commercial Updating)
Adult Training Promotions Unit, Room 2/2, Department of Education and Science, Elizabeth House, York Road, London SE1 7PH
071-934 0888

Rapid Results College
Tuition House, 27–37 St George's Road, London SW19 4DS
081-947 2211
Courses by correspondence. This is an accredited correspondence college.

Registrar of Companies
Companies House, Crown Way, Maindy, Cardiff CF4 3UZ
0222 388588

Holds the data on UK limited companies. A source of information. Supplies company information for a fee, providing a useful source of comparison with your own results.

Rural Development Commission
141 Castle Street, Salisbury, Wiltshire SP1 3TP
0722 336255

Offers advice, help, courses and finance in English rural areas, that is towns with a population below 10,000.

The Small Firms Service
Operates in many parts of the country, controlled by the Department of Employment. Telephone the operator on 100 and ask for Freefone Enterprise. An advisory and counselling service is also available from approximately 80 **Training and Enterprise Councils** (TECs) in England and Wales. Those already set up are listed below, by region.

Tourist boards
Offer help, advice and financial support for tourism projects.

English Tourist Board
Thames Tower, Blacks Road, London W6 9EL
081-846 9000

Scottish Tourist Board
Croythorn House, 23 Ravelston Terrace, Edinburgh EH4 3EU
031-332 2433

Wales Tourist Board
Brunel House, 2 Fitzallen Road, Cardiff CF2 1UY
0222 499909

Training and Enterprise Council (TEC offices)

South East
Essex TEC, Employment Department: Training Agency, Globe House, New Street, Chelmsford, Essex CM1 1UG

Hampshire TEC, Projects Office, Home Farm, Leigh Road, Eastleigh, Hampshire SO5 4EU

Hertfordshire TEC, New Barnes Mill, Cotton Mill Lane, St Albans, Herts AL1 2HA

Isle of Wight TEC, Isle of Wight Development Board, Samuel White Boardroom, 40 Medina Road, Cowes, Isle of Wight PO31 7LP

Kent TEC, c/o Employment Department Training Agency, 5th Floor, Mountbatten House, 28 Military Road, Chatham, Kent ME4 4JE

London
AZTEC, Manorgate House, 2 Manorgate Road, Kingston-upon-Thames, Surrey KT2 7AL

London East TEC, c/o East London Area Office, Cityside House, 40 Adler Street, London E1 1EE

South London TEC, c/o South London Area Office, Skyline House, 200 Union Street, London SE1 0LX

Milton Keynes & North Bucks TEC, c/o Skillscentre, Chesney Wold, Bleak Hall, Milton Keynes, Bucks MK6 1LX

Oxfordshire
Heart of England TEC, c/o Employment Department: Training Agency, 26/27 The Quadrant, Abingdon Science Park, off Barton Lane, Abingdon OX14 3YS

Surrey TEC, c/o Employment Department: Training Agency, Surrey Area Office, Technology House, 48–54 Goldsworth Road, Woking, Surrey GU21 1LE

Sussex TEC, c/o Employment Department: Training Agency, Sussex Area Office, Gresham House, 12–24 Station Road, Crawley, West Sussex RH10 1HT

Thames Valley Enterprise TEC, 6th Floor, Kings Point, 120 Kings Road, Reading RG1 3BZ

South West
Avon TEC, c/o Employment Department, Training Agency, Minster House, 27 Baldwin Street, Bristol BS99 7HR

Devon & Cornwall TEC, 6th Floor, Tower Block, North Road, BR Station, Plymouth PL4 AA

Dorset TEC, 1st Floor, Bracken House, 14–16 Christchurch Road, Bournemouth BH1 3NN

Gloucestershire TEC, c/o Employment Department: Training Agency, Conway House, 33–35 Worcester Street, Gloucester GL1 3AJ

Somerset TEC, c/o Employment Department: Training Agency, Somerset Area Office, Crescent House, 3–7 The Mount, Taunton, Somerset TA1 3TT

West Midlands
Employment Department: Training Agency, 16th Floor Metropolitan House, 1 Hagley Road, Birmingham B16 8TG

Coventry
Employment Department: Training Agency, Coventry & Warwickshire Area Office, 6th Floor, Bankfield House, 163 New Union Street, Coventry CV1 2QQ

Dudley TEC, c/o Employment Department: Training Agency, 5th Floor, Flacon House, The Minories, Dudley DY2 8PG

Redditch
CENTEC, Unit 21, Greenlands Business Centre, Studley Road, Redditch B98 7HF

Sandwell TEC, William King Ltd, Atlas Centre, Union Road, West Bromwich, West Midlands B70 0DR

Staffordshire TEC, c/o Employment Department: Training Agency, Moorlands House, 24 Trinity Street, Hanley, Stoke-on-Trent ST1 5LN

Walsall TEC, c/o InterTAN UK Ltd, Tandy Centre, Leamore Lane, Bloxwich, Walsall WS2 7PS

Wolverhampton TEC, Wobaston Road, Ford Houses, Wolverhampton WV10 6AJ

Worcester
HAWTEC, Hazwell House, Sansom Street, Worcester WR1 1UH

East Midlands and East Anglia
Bedfordshire TEC, c/o TA Bedfordshire & Cambridgeshire Area Office, Wesley House, 19 Chapel Street, Luton LU1 2SE

Central & South Cambridgeshire TEC, Carlyle House, Carlyle Road, Cambridge CB4 3DN

North Derbyshire TEC, c/o TA Derby Area Office, St Peters House, Gower Street, Derby DE1 1SB

Southern Derbyshire TEC, c/o TA Derby Area Office, St Peters House, Gower Street, Derby DE1 1SB

Lincolnshire TEC, c/o Employment Department: Training Agency, Lincolnshire Area Office, Wigford House, Brayford Wharf East, Lincoln LN5 7AY

Norfolk & Waveney TEC, 112 Barrack Street, Norwich NR3 1UB

Northamptonshire TEC, c/o The Training Shop, 85–87 Weedon Road, Northamptonshire NN5 5BG

Great Nottingham TEC, c/o Employment Department: Training Agency, Nottingham Area Office, Lambert House, Talbot Street, Nottingham NG1 5GL

North Nottinghamshire TEC, Edwinstowe Hall College, Church Street, Edwinstowe, Mansfield NG21 9QA

Greater Peterborough TEC, c/o Skills Training Agency, Saville Road, Westwood, Peterborough PE3 6TQ

Suffolk TEC, c/o Employment Department: Training Agency, 2nd Floor Crown House, Crown Street, Ipswich IP1 3HS

Yorkshire and Humberside
Barnsley/Doncaster TEC, c/o Employment Department: Training Agency, Conference Centre, Eldon Street, Barnsley S70 2TN

Bradford & District TEC, c/o TA Bradford Area Office, 5th Floor, Provincial House, Bradford BD1 1NW

Calderdale & Kirklees TEC, 5th Floor Provincial House, Tyrell Street, Bradford BD1 1NW

Humberside TEC, c/o Employment Department: Training Agency, Humberside Area Office, 4th Floor, Essex House, Manor Street, Hull HU1 1YA

Leeds TEC, c/o Employment Department: Training Agency, Leeds Area Office, Fairfax House, Merrion Street, Leeds LS2 8LH

North Yorkshire TEC, c/o Employment Department: Training Agency, 4th Floor, Fairfax House, Merrion Street, Leeds LS2 8LH

Rotherham TEC, c/o Employment Department: Training Agency, Chesham House, Charter Row, Sheffield S1 3EB

Sheffield TEC, c/o Employment Department: Training Agency, 1st Floor, Don House, The Pennine Centre, 20–22 Hawley Street, Sheffield S1 3GA

Wakefield TEC, c/o Employment Department: Training Agency, York House, 31–36 York Place, Leeds LS1 2EB

North West
Bolton/Bury TEC, c/o Employment Department: Training Agency, Manchester North Area Office, Bayley House, St Georges Square, Bolton BL1 2HB

CEWTEC, c/o Cavendish Enterprise Ltd, Brassey Street, Off Laird Street, Birkenhead, Wirral L41 8BY

Cumbria TEC, Venture House, Regents Court, Guard Street, Cumbria CA14 4EW

Lancashire
ELTEC Ltd, Suite 506, Glenfield Park, Site 2 Northrop Avenue, Blackburn BB1 5QF

Lancashire Area West
LAWTEC Development Ltd, c/o TA Lancashire Area Office, 4th Floor Duchy House, 96 Lancaster Road, Preston PR1 1HE

Manchester
Manchester TEC, c/o Employment Department: Training Agency, 2nd Floor, 25 Aytoun Street, Manchester M60 7HS

Merseyside TEC, c/o Employment Department: Training Agency, Merseyside Area Office, 3rd Floor Tithebarn House, Tithebarn Street, Liverpool L2 2NZ

Oldham TEC Development Ltd, Block D 3rd Floor, Brunswick Square, Union Street, Oldham OL1 1DE

Rochdale TEC, St James Place, 160–162 Yorkshire Street, Rochdale, Lancashire OL16 2DL

Cheshire
South & East Cheshire TEC, PO Box 37, Beta Road, Off Brooks Lane, Middlewich, Cheshire CW10 0QE

St Helens
Qualitec (St Helens) Ltd, Rainford Council Offices, Church Road, Rainford, St Helens, Merseyside WA11 8HB

Stockport/High Peak TEC, c/o Buckleys, Welkin Mill, Welkin Road, Bredbury, Stockport SK6 2BL

Wigan

METROTEC (Wigan) Ltd, c/o Read Corrugated Cases, Warrington Road, Goose Green, Wigan WN3 6XD

Northern

County Durham TEC, Employment Department: Training Agency, Valley Street North, Darlington DL1 1JT

Northumberland TEC, Employment Department: Training Agency, Wellbar House, Gallowgate, Newcastle upon Tyne NE1 4TF

Teesside TEC, Corporation House, 73 Albert Road, Middlesbrough, Cleveland TS1 2RU

Tyneside TEC, Moongate House, 5th Avenue Business Park, Team Valley Trading Estate, Gateshead NE11 0HF

Wearside TEC, Derwent House, New Town Centre, Washington, Tyne and Wear NE38 7ST

Wales

Gwent

Employment Department: Training Agency, Gwent TEC Development Unit, Tredegar Park, Newport, Gwent NP1 9XA

Mid-Glamorgan TEC, Tudor Jenkins Building, Cowbridge Road, Talbot Green, Pontyclun, Mid-Glamorgan CF7 8HL

North East Wales TEC, World Help Ltd, 2nd Floor, Centenary Building, King Street, Wrexham, Clwyd LL13 1HH

North West Wales TEC, Development Unit, 1st Floor, Bron Castell, High Street, Bangor, Gwynedd LL57 1YS

Powys TEC, Development Team, Courtyard Restaurant Offices, 2nd Floor, Parkers Lane, Newtown, Powys

South Glamorgan TEC, 5th Floor, Phase 1 Buildings, Government Buildings, Tyglas, Llanishen, Cardiff CF4 3PJ

West Wales TEC, 1 Tawe Business Village, Phoenix Way, Enterprise Park, Swansea, West Glamorgan

West Wales TEC, 1 Tawe Business Village, Tyglas, Llanishen, Cardiff CF4 3PJ

Chapter 3: Six Months Before Start-Up

The Business Plan Workbook, Colin and Paul Barrow, 1988.

How to Choose Business Premises, Howard Green, Brian Chalkley and Paul Foley, 1986.

How to Prepare a Business Plan, Edward Blackwell, 1989.

Practical Marketing, David H Bangs, 1990.
A manual to help business owners put together a goal-orientated, resource-based marketing plan; includes worksheet and checklists at every stage to make implementation and review easier.

Chapter 4: Four Months Before Start-Up

Annual Abstract of Statistics, No 125, HMSO, 1990.

Census of Population (1981 census), HMSO.

Getting Started, Robson Rhodes, 2nd edition, 1990

Guide to Official Statistics, No 6, HMSO, 1989.

Regional Trends, No 24, HMSO, 1989.

Starting a Successful Small Business, M J Morris, 2nd edition, 1989.

Chapter 5: Three Months Before Start-Up

How to Deal with Your Bank Manager, Geoffrey Sales, 1988.

Wages Councils
Wages Councils issue Orders affecting basic pay, weekly hours and holiday entitlement as they apply to certain industries and trades; the terms apply to workers over 21 years old. Copies of Wages Orders are available from Steel House, 11 Tothill Street, London SW1H 9NF.

It is an offence to pay less than the minimum specified in the relevant Wages Order, which must be displayed on your premises.

Chapter 6: Two Months Before Start-Up

Be Your Own PR Man, Michael Bland, 2nd edition, 1987.

Do Your Own Market Research, Paul N Hague and Peter Jackson, 1988.

Effective Interviewing, John Fletcher, 1988.

Employment Law for the Small Business, Anne Knell, 1989.

How to Do Marketing Research, Paul N Hague and Peter Jackson, 1990.

Making Marketing Work, Patrick Forsyth and Gerard Earls, 1989.

Practical Marketing, David H Bangs, 1990

Running Your Own Shop, Roger Cox, 2nd edition, 1989.

Chapter 7: **One Month Before Start-Up**

Customer Service, Malcolm Peel, 1988.

Chapter 8: **Start-Up and After**

Going for Growth, Michael K Lawson, 1988.

Make Every Minute Count, Marion E Haynes, 1989.

Managing Your Time, Lothar J Seiwert, 1989.

Successful Expansion for the Small Business, M J Morris, 1984.

◀ APPENDIX 3 ▶

GLOSSARY OF FINANCIAL TERMS

If you are new to financial statements, the following operational definitions will help you become familiar with financial jargon.

'Acid Test' Ratio. Cash, plus other assets which can be immediately converted to cash, should equal or exceed current liabilities. The formula used to determine the ratio is as follows:

$$\frac{\text{Cash} + \text{Debtors} + \text{Marketable Securities}}{\text{Current Liabilities}}$$

The acid test ratio is one of the most important credit barometers used by lending institutions, as it indicates the ability of a business enterprise to meet its current obligations.

Aging Debtors. A scheduling of debtors according to the length of time they have been outstanding. This shows which accounts are not being paid on time and may reveal any difficulty in collecting long-overdue debts. This may also be an important indicator of developing cash flow problems.

Amortisation. To liquidate on an instalment basis; the process of gradually paying off a liability over a period, eg a mortgage is amortised by periodically paying off part of the capital amount of the mortgage.

Assets. The valuable resources, or properties and property rights owned by an individual or business.

Balance sheet. An itemised statement which lists the total assets, liabilities, and net worth of a business to reflect its financial condition at a given moment.

Bought ledger. Goods bought on credit by the business. Also called *purchase ledger*.

Capital. Capital funds are those funds which are needed for the base of the business. Usually they are put into the business in a fairly permanent form such as fixed assets, plant and equipment, or are used in other ways which are not recoverable in the short term unless the entire business is sold.

Capital equipment. Equipment used to manufacture a product, provide a service, or to sell, store and deliver merchandise. Such equipment will not be sold in the normal course of business, but will be used and worn out or be consumed over time as business is conducted.

Cash flow. The actual movement of cash within a business: cash inflow minus cash outflow. A term used to designate the reported net income of a company plus amounts charged for depreciation, depletion, amortisation and extraordinary charges to reserves, which are book-keeping deductions and not actually paid out in cash. Used to offer a better indication of the ability of a firm to meet its own obligations and to pay dividends, rather than the conventional net income figure.

Cash from sales. Credit sales, where payment is postponed and you effectively grant credit to your customers, and which will (we hope) eventually turn to cash. The decision to grant credit is a deeply involved and difficult one, and many business owners prefer not to issue credit themselves, but rather dump the decision on to a bank by using one or more of the major credit cards. Before you decide to issue credit, discuss the advisability of such a move with your bank manager and other financial advisers. You may find that competitive considerations force you to offer credit.

Cash position. See *Liquidity*.

Collateral. An asset pledged to a lender in order to support the loan.

Cumulative Cash Flow. For the first month, equals net cash flow. For subsequent months, equals previous month's cumulative cash flow plus new month's net cash flow. This is a particularly important figure, because it is used to calculate new capital and debt needs well in advance of the time those monies are needed in the business. If you can show a CCF to your bank and explain why you will need a loan five months hence, your chances of business success are greatly improved.

Current assets. Cash or other items that will normally be turned into cash within one year, and assets that will be used up in the operations of a firm within one year.

Current liabilities. Amounts owed that will ordinarily be paid by a firm within one year. Such items include bought ledger, wages, taxes, the current portion of a long-term debt, and interest and dividends payable.

Current ratio. A ratio of a firm's current assets to its current liabilities. Because a current ratio includes the value of stock that has not yet been sold, it does not offer the best evaluation of the firm's current status. The *acid test ratio*, covering the most liquid of current assets, produces a better evaluation.

Debt. Debt refers to borrowed funds, whether from your own coffers or from other individuals, banks or institutions. It is generally secured with a note, which in turn may be secured by a lien against property or other assets. Ordinarily, the note states repayment and interest provisions, which vary greatly in both amount and duration, depending upon the purpose, source, and terms of the loan. Some debt is convertible, that is, it may be changed into direct ownership of a portion of a business under certain stated conditions.

Debtors. Those who owe money to a business. Customers' accounts will be referred to as sales ledger.

Drawings. A major problem for small businesses is that the owners take out too much in salary, advances, and even loans from the company to themselves. A red flag to your bank manager and other creditors.

Equipment. Usually limited to equipment used in the operation of the business.

Equity. Equity is the owner's investment in the business. Unlike capital, equity is what remains after the liabilities of the company are subtracted from the assets – thus it may be greater than or less than the capital invested in the business. Equity investment carries with it a share of ownership and usually a share in profits, as well as some say in how the business is managed.

149

Goodwill. Excess of purchase price over book value (net worth minus subordinated debt) of the business. Applies only to a business which is purchased.

Gross profit. Net sales (sales minus returned merchandise, discounts, or other allowances) minus the cost of goods sold.

Guarantee. A pledge by a third party to repay a loan in the event the borrower cannot.

Income statement. A statement of income and expenses for a given period of time.

Limited company. A legal entity, separate from its owners. Profits and losses are the company's and it has its own debts and obligations. The business continues following the resignation, death or bankruptcy of the management and the shareholders.

Liquidity. A term used to describe the solvency of a business, and which has special reference to the degree of readiness with which assets can be converted into cash without loss. Also called *cash position*. If a firm's current assets cannot be converted into cash to meet current liabilities, the firm is said to be *illiquid*.

Loan agreement. A document which states what a business can or cannot do as long as it owes money to (usually) a bank. A loan agreement may place restrictions on the owner's salary, or dividends, on amount of other debt, on working capital, on sales, or on the number of additional personnel.

Loans. Debt money for private business is usually in the form of bank loans, which, in a sense, are personal because a private business can be harder to evaluate in terms of creditworthiness and degree of risk. A secured loan is a loan which is backed up by a claim against some asset or assets of a business. An unsecured loan is backed by the faith the bank has in the borrower's ability to pay back the money.

Long-term liabilities. These are liabilities (expenses) which will not mature within the next year.

Net worth. The owner's equity in a given business represented by the excess of the total assets over the total amounts owed to outside creditors (total liabilities) at a given moment. Also, the net worth of an individual as determined by deducting the amount of all his or her personal liabilities from the total value of his personal assets. Generally refers to tangible net worth, ie does not include goodwill, etc.

Partnership. A legal relationship created by the voluntary association of two or more persons to carry on as co-owners of a business for profit; a type of business organisation in which two or more persons agree on the amount of their contributions (capital and effort) and on the distribution of profits, if any.

Profit. The excess of the selling price over all costs and expenses incurred in making a sale. Also, the reward to the entrepreneur for the risks assumed by him or her in the establishment, operations, and management of a given enterprise or undertaking.

Purchase ledger. See *Bought ledger*.

Reserves. One of your goals – to build tax-advantaged value in your business – is to retain the earnings in the business (in new assets, lower liabilities, and cash or cash equivalents). Ask your accountant about this if you find you have a lot of earnings to retain. There are tax implications. A negative reserves figure alarms your bank and other creditors, and is usually a sign that more capital is needed if the business is to survive and prosper.

Sales ledger. Customers who have bought on credit.

Sole trader. A type of business organisation in which one individual owns the business. Legally, the owner *is* the business and personal assets are typically exposed to liabilities of the business.

Stock. The materials owned and held by a business, including new materials, intermediate products and parts, work-in-progress and finished goods, intended either for internal consumption or for sale.

Take-over. The acquisition of one company by another.

Target market. The *specific* individuals, distinguished by socio-economic, demographic, and/or interest characteristics, who are the most likely potential customers for the goods and/or services of a business.

Term loans. Either secured or unsecured, usually for periods of more than a year to as many as 10. Term loans are paid off like a mortgage: so much per month for so many years. The most common uses of term loans are for equipment and other fixed asset purposes, for working capital, and for property.

Working capital. The difference between current assets and current liabilities. Contrasted with capital, a permanent use of funds, working capital cycles through your business in a variety of forms: stock, accounts and debtors, and cash and securities.

◀ INDEX ▶

add = address

References in italics indicate figures or tables